MW01063192

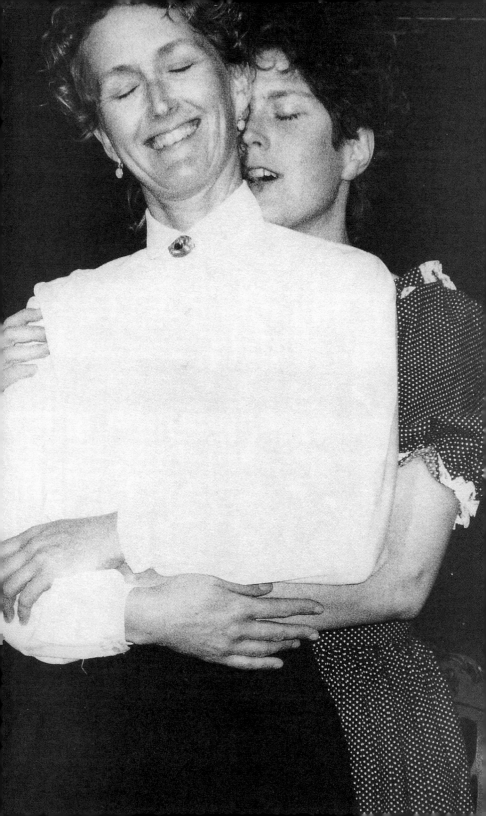

The Second Coming of Joan of Arc and Other Plays

by Carolyn Gage

The Second Coming of Joan of Arc and Other Plays by Carolyn Gage. Copyright © 1994 by Carolyn Gage. All rights whatsoever in these plays are strictly reserved. Applications for performance, including professional, amateur, motion pictures, recitation, lecturing, public reading, broadcasting, television, and the rights of translation into foreign languages, should be addressed to the playwright care of HerBooks, P.O. Box 7467, Santa Cruz, CA 95061.

Printed in the United States of America by McNaughton and Gunn. ISBN: 0-939821-06-0

Cover photo: Carolyn Gage in *The Second Coming of Joan of Arc*. Photo by Linda J. Russell. All other photos by Tarascon.

Title page photo: *"Let me love you, Louisa!"* A passionate Jo March (Sue Carney) attempts to seduce her famous creator, Louisa May Alcott (Michaelia Morgan) in *Louisa May Incest*.

Louisa May Incest was originally published in *Trivia*, vol. 17, 1990.

The Second Coming of Joan of Arc was originally published in *Sinister Wisdom*, #3, Summer/Fall 1988.

Dedication

To the courageous and talented women of No to Men Productions, who first brought these characters to life on the stage.

Acknowledgements:

I would like to thank Pauline Peotter, who taught me the Craft of playwriting and who en-Couraged me to take myself seriously. It was because of her interest and support that I wrote my first plays.

I also wish to thank Hyacinth Ware, a good friend and intrepid stage manager, who stood by me through all the storms. The story of No to Men Productions and of the lives of the women who made up the company deserves a book in itself. To all of the women who lost their jobs, their homes, their families, their friends, and their mental and physical health because of their participation in the theatre—thank you. A special thanks to Sue Carney, Tere Knight, Krystal Locke, Sue Lundquist, Michaelia Morgan, Akia Woods, and Wyrda.

Finally, my gratitude to Irene Reti who believed in the plays enough to publish them, and to De Clarke, for her thoughtful comments on the original draft.

—*Carolyn Gage*

HerBooks would like to particularly thank De Clarke for her editorial assistance on this collection. Many thanks also to Kathy Miriam, Shoney Sien and Gloria Anzaldúa. And, as always, thanks to Julia Chapin, whose proofreading and editorial skills are a blessing to all HerBooks titles.

Table of Contents

Cast members of *Louisa May Incest* and *Battered on Broadway* take a bow: Judy Kaplan, Wyrda, Sue Carney, Michaelia Morgan, Natalie Garrett, Akia Woods, and Carolyn Gage.

Introduction

I am an actor, and I wrote these plays for actors—especially for the women who have been relegated to the ranks of "character actors" because of our lack of conformity to the rigid standards for women in the dominant culture.

Open casting is not enough. It may enhance opportunities for formerly marginalized women to gain experience and exposure, but we will never be able to achieve greatness in our art until we have a strong canon of plays where the roles for women are written by, for, and serve the interests of ourselves and a culture of women.

The Second Coming of Joan of Arc gives voice to a character conspicuous in her absence from heteropatriarchal theatre: the angry young woman. This Joan of Arc is a far cry from the eroticized and idealized Joan of Anouihl or Shaw. This Joan, like the historical one, is a teenager, a runaway from an alcoholic home with an incestuous father, a girl with severe eating disorders, and a lesbian. No longer a martyr and a victim, this Joan redeems her experience through unmasking her betrayers and rallying contemporary women with a rousing call to arms.

The Roar of Silence is a trilogy of one-acts about prominent lesbians from the past who are confronted with histories of sexual abuse. *Mason-Dixon*, an exposé of "smiling racism," explores the interface of race, class, and gender between a white woman and a formerly enslaved African-American woman who shared intimacies as children. *Jane Addams and the Devil Baby* brings an elderly Irish emigrant with traditional Catholic values into conflict with the famous lesbian who founded the first settlement house. In *Louisa May Incest*, I was interested in the problems confronting the writer who ventures into areas in her work which are taboo in her personal life. In this case, Louisa May Alcott has created a lesbian alter-ego as the main character of her most famous novel, and now in being true to her vision, Louisa is threatened with uncovering her own repressed lesbianism and experiences of incest.

Battered on Broadway, subtitled "A Vendetta in One Act," was written to exorcise my own ambivalence about the old Broadway musicals. As a playwright and lyricist, I have had to spend hundreds of hours researching and dissecting these scripts and scores, and they have been a tremendous source of joy and inspiration. They have also been a source of rage and sadness, as I have had to pick my way around and sort through the toxic values represented in the plots and characters. *Battered on Broadway* was an act of deliberate appropriation—but it also goes beyond the issue of Broadway misogyny to address the problems between women of different class and ethnic backgrounds when we attempt to formulate a common strategy for dealing with the violence against us.

The last two plays in the collection are one-woman shows, giving the spotlight to women who are seldom granted serious treatment in theatre: the alcoholic butch, and the poverty-class woman who has been labeled criminally insane.

In *Calamity Jane Sends a Message to Her Daughter*, I am interested in the real Calamity, not the Doris Day version. And the real Calamity is a type familiar to any woman who haunts the women's bars. She is the older alcoholic butch, with the devastating sense of humor—often making herself the butt of her jokes, but taking deadly aim at the hypocrisies of a society which has systematically robbed her of status and dignity, even while it has elevated the men with whom she has matched achievements.

Cookin' with Typhoid Mary gives the floor to the enigmatic Mary Mallon, the woman who steadfastly denied the existence of germs and refused to cooperate with the public health authorities, even though her resistance would cost her her freedom. As Mary unfolds her story of life as a poverty-class Irish emigrant on the streets of New York, her so-called paranoia takes on a different cast, and the real public enemy becomes defined as a government which cared more for the lives of five wealthy typhoid victims than for the starvation of half of Ireland.

May these plays find their way into the hands of actors, especially lesbian actors, who have been frustrated and stunted by the narrow range of roles for women and who have felt we were contributing to our own oppression by perpetuating views of the world which erased or trivialized our own existence. And may these plays also find their way into the hands of those women who, alienated by what they have seen on the contemporary stage, might never have considered their own potential as dramatic artists.

—*Carolyn Gage*

The Second Coming
of Joan of Arc

THE SECOND COMING OF JOAN OF ARC

Prologue

Okay. Here it is. Here's Compiègne over here. It's ours. And there's Margny, over there. It belongs to the Duke of Burgundy's men. Those are the French who are fighting for the English king—you know, the "enemy." And here's the river in the middle. And over the river is a bridge, right from Compiègne to Margny. And this bridge is unguarded. All we have to do is cross over, surprise them, and Margny's ours. Nothing to it, right?

So that's what we do . . . almost. We cross, we attack, they retreat. And then suddenly off over here, we see more of the Duke of Burgundy's men coming from the next town across the way. Well, I mean that's not good news, but it's not the end of the world either. I say to myself, "This is going to take a little longer than I thought." But my soldiers? They see these reinforcements, and you know what they do? They lose it. Completely. They take off running back across the bridge to Compiègne, and I'm yelling at them and trying to get them to stand and fight, but there's no way to stop them. Did you ever try to stop a scared man? Yeah, right. So I do the next best thing. I stay behind and cover their retreat.

So here I am, on my horse, fighting backwards to get across the bridge, with all my soldiers streaming past me, and suddenly, I hear this terrible noise—chhhh!—I mean, it is the worst noise in the world—CHHHHHHHH!

5

You know what that is? That's the sound the drawbridge at Compiègne makes when it's being raised—by my own men!

So, here I am, cut off, surrounded by enemy soldiers. Yeah, I'm "captured." I think the word is "ditched."

You know, when you're locked in a cell for eight months with nothing to do, you have a lot of time to ask yourself questions. Questions like, "Why the hell didn't they wait to raise that lousy drawbridge?" Don't tell me they didn't know where I was. The entire army had to run past me on the bridge to get to Compiègne. And don't tell me they thought I could take care of myself. Me, against five hundred soldiers?

Come on, what were they thinking? You know what I decided? I decided they weren't thinking at all, which in itself is a statement. They were scared. They were in a hurry. They saw me fighting on the bridge, but they didn't think about it. They did not think about what would happen to me if they raised the drawbridge. It was irrelevant.

You know, there is a term for the chapters on women in your high school history books: "nonessential information." In the brains of these men, the textbook of their personal history has two essential chapters—the one on fraternity and the one on chivalry. The chapter on fraternity tells them how to act around other men—how to be a team player, a loyal comrade, an esteemed colleague. It tells them to close ranks against outsiders and never, ever, under any circumstances to desert a brother officer in the heat of battle. The chapter on chivalry tells them that if they're on a sinking ship, they should make sure the women and children are saved first.

But you see, I was neither a brother, nor a helpless female. In the textbook of their brains, the section on me was just an insert—with a border of little cannons around it, and a heading in flowery letters, "The Maid of Orléans." It was nonessential information. They would not be held responsible for it during a test. So, with the enemy bearing down on them, they stuck to the essentials. The image of me still fighting on the bridge was entered into their programs for fraternity and chivalry, but nothing turned up—so they raised the drawbridge.

Now, in case you're thinking this kind of thing only happens to butch women—I say, look again. I submit that every one of you is an insert in the textbook of your country. I look out over this sea of nonessential faces, and I can see the little borders around your lives, individually and collectively. You are inserts in the lives of men. You are inserts in the history of your nation. You are inserts in the roll book of your government. And when it comes down to the real issues, we will all be missing from the program—CHHHHH!

What I am here for tonight is to take the border off "Saint Joan of Arc," and to put my life back into the main text. My story is not a sidelight of history, some piece of local color, optional reading. My story is the story of all women, and my suffering is *identical* to yours. My trial is the trial of all women. My misguided crusade is all of our misguided crusades. My enemies are your enemies. My mistakes are your mistakes. The voices I hear are your voices. And the voices you hear are my voices.

Part I

In the first place, my name is not Joan. It's Jeanne. So how did "Jeanne" get to be "Joan?" It got lost in the translation. In five hundred years, a lot of things about my life got lost in the translation.

In the second place, "of Arc" makes it sound like I come from a town called "Arc." I don't. I come from Domremy. There's no such place as "Arc." It's a poor translation of my father's name—and besides that, I never used his name. I went by my mother's name, Romée.

7

And in the third place, I never gave anybody permission to make me a saint. Think about it. The same boys that burned me at the stake want to turn around and make me a public relations officer for their church! Right. Over my dead body.

So I'm not "Saint Joan of Arc." I'm Jeanne Romée. Big deal, right? Who cares? I care! Joan of Arc is *not* my name, and "saint" is just another word for a woman who got burned, and it's time we woke up and stopped letting other people change our names, and it's time we stopped believing it's some kind of honor to be tortured by men—and most of all, it's time we started telling the truth about our own lives. These myths are killing us!

So . . . soldier, martyr, hero, saint. All between the ages of seventeen and nineteen. That is when I died. Nineteen. I just had those two years. Soldier, martyr, hero, saint. Idiot.

It was my death that really did it. The beautiful young peasant girl clutching a makeshift cross, eyes lifted up to heaven, as she disappears in a cloud of fiery smoke. That was the death of "Saint Joan of Arc." Tonight I want to tell you how Jeanne Romée died.

The beginning of the end was Easter Day, 1430. I was all of eighteen. The city of Mélun had just surrendered to me, which was very exciting, because it had belonged to the Duke of Burgundy for ten years. I was standing on the walls of the city, and the soldiers and the people were all cheering me, and the bells of the church were all ringing for Easter. I couldn't have been happier. The king had been crowned, I was a national hero, everything was possible. And then I heard my voices.

My voices. Everyone always wants to know about my voices. When do I hear them? What do they sound like? Do other people hear them too? And here's my favorite one from the English: "So . . . how come they speak to you in French?"

My voices weren't all that special. Everybody hears voices. Everybody's got somebody leaning over their shoulder, whispering in their ear what they should do and what they shouldn't do. You know, "Get the hair out of your face! Put your knees together!" That's what civilization's all about, isn't it, listening to the voices of those who lived before you did? That's what keeps the whole machinery going. No, the real problem for civilization comes when a woman decides to invent her own voices and then believe in them. See, that's almost like thinking for yourself.

You're surprised to hear me say I invented my voices? Let's put it this way—I heard what I believed as much as I believed what I heard. I mean, think about it. Where is the reality in the voices *you* hear? Is it "out there" somewhere, or do you make it real for yourself? Just where does the authority come from? Hey, come on, we all invent our voices. Mine were just more blatantly fictional, that's all. And that is because I didn't like the selection available to young women in Domremy.

There was my father's voice: "Jeanne, a rich young man will come and marry you and you will go and live with him and he will help your poor old father take care of his sheep." And then there was my mother: "Jeanne, a nice young man will come and marry you and you will go and have lots of babies and then you will understand exactly how I feel." Oh, and let's not forget the priest: "Jeanne, God has called you to give yourself to him and you will go and enter a convent and say prayers all day long that things will get better." All the voices in Domremy were more or less variations on these themes.

But then one day, I'm walking in my father's garden and I hear, "Jeanne! You have been chosen by God to ride at the head of the army, to take the king to be crowned, and to drive the English out of France!" Yeah . . . Now that's what I call a voice. It was the voice of St. Michael, and I liked it so much, a few days later I heard St. Catherine and St. Margaret.

So why saints, and why these particular saints? Well, you have to remember that Domremy was a pretty small place, and good role models were hard to come by. I mean, outside your family and your neighbors, you were pretty much looking at the sheep. If I wanted another point of reference, I was going to have to use my imagination—and I did. There was a statue of St. Margaret in our church, and there was one of St. Catherine in the church across the river, and everybody knew who St. Michael was, because he was the patron saint of the district, so not too surprisingly, these were my role models, my "voices."

Let me tell you about them. First there was St. Michael. He led an army of angels out to do battle with Satan, and kicked him out of heaven. He was our Catholic cowboy, our superhero saint. He always wore full armor and carried a sword.

Then there was St. Catherine. She was arrested and put on trial for her religious beliefs. Fifty old men sat around and asked her a lot of trick questions, but she outsmarted them all, which turned out not to be so smart, because it made her sexually irresistible to the Emperor who had had her arrested in the first place. And of course, he had to do something to save face when she turned him down, so he cut off her head.

And then there was St. Margaret. You're going to like her. She ran away the night she was supposed to get married, and she cut her hair very short and passed herself off as a monk for many years. Now, this worked out fine, until some woman came along and accused her of getting her pregnant. Way to go, Margaret! But then, Margaret decided it was better to spend the rest of her life in solitary confinement than to admit she was a woman. But they found out anyway and cut off her head.

Some role models, right? Michael, Catherine, Margaret. And guess what? I grew up to lead an army, dress like a man, and stand trial for my religious beliefs. No, my life wasn't original at all. I copied my role models just as faithfully as any one of you copy yours. Mine were just a little more flamboyant.

We have *got* to stop and take a look at our role models! Like maybe just spend two minutes thinking about the people we're going to spend the next fifty years imitating? Take me for instance. I had two female martyrs, both beheaded, and one male conquering hero. What I should have noticed was that the only happy ending was the man's. What I should have also noticed was that a conquering male gets a whole different reception than a conquering female. And that is because the only thing a woman is expected to defeat is herself. Anything else is not victory, but castration. What I'm saying is that I should have noticed I had a third act that wouldn't work. The lead part was written for a man.

What, and I mean *what*, is the happy ending for women? Marriage, where the whole company comes out onstage and joins hands around the happy couple while they ring down the curtain? And they better ring it down at this point, because, as we all know, that's when the leading lady retires from the stage.

Or is the happy ending those scenes where the fatally wounded or terminally ill heroine sings her dying aria in the arms of her broken-hearted lover? The bad news is she dies, but the good news is he really did love her after all—too little, too late maybe—but, hey, who's keeping score?

Is there some happy ending for us that doesn't call for our total spiritual annihilation? What if we all dropped everything—whatever we've got going right now—what if we just *stopped* until we could figure out what that happy ending is? And not just figure it out, but see it, feel it, touch it, taste it! Because I am here to tell you, you are going to paint what you're looking at, and if we don't come up with something better than these martyred female saints, we're all going to end up at the stake. Today you women are allowed to go out and work in the men's world, but when I did it back in 1430, I was a real freak. But the men haven't changed, the rules haven't changed, and the institutions haven't changed.

The fact that there are more of us doing it, just means they're getting ready to build a bigger fire.

But, getting back to the voices. . . . The first time I heard them I was thirteen. That's a good age for internalizing voices, isn't it? The age of puberty.

Puberty. I knew all about puberty even before I got there, because I had figured out it was the missing link in the story of my mother's life. Isabella Romée was my mother. I didn't see too much of her, even though I lived under the same roof with her for seventeen years—if you know what I mean. By the time I was born, she had already had three kids and spent more than half her life married. Any time she opened her mouth, it was either wife-talk or mother-talk. The only time I ever heard Isabella speak with her own voice was when she would tell us kids about her trip to Rome.

When she was a girl, her family had gone on a pilgrimage to see the Pope, and they had taken her along. It was a big adventure—traveling all that way, going into a foreign country, staying in a different place every night, camping out, meeting all kinds of people from all kinds of places. Whenever she told us these stories, she would get very animated, and her eyes would shine, and she would literally turn into somebody else—somebody I never knew, somebody who never had children, somebody who had lived another whole life in another whole world. And this person who had had all these adventures, and who wanted to go back again, and who was brave and independent and funny—well, she was not my mother.

The only thing I could figure out was that something terrible, I mean *really* terrible, must have happened to turn this girl with all the big adventures into this woman who would be doing the exact same things tomorrow that she did yesterday. I didn't know what this terrible thing was, until I saw it happen to my big sister. In one year, she went from being full of crazy ideas and lots of fun, to being somebody serious and

12

boring and busy. The terrible thing was puberty, and I made up my mind it was never going to happen to me.

Puberty. The beginning of periods, which means you can have babies. The beginning of breasts, which means you can nurse babies. The beginning of feeling self-conscious around boys, because you have this opening between your legs they all want to stick themselves into.

Puberty is about loss of privacy. It's about living in a body which has become public property. It's about foreign invasion, about occupied territory. One by one, my girlfriends surrendered themselves. I watched them go off with boys and turn themselves into foreigners—Mengette, Charlotte, and even my best friend Hauviette—or at least that's what I thought at the time . . . but that's a whole other story.

Every day I could feel my family, my relatives, my neighbors laying siege to me. They surrounded me, and they would not let anything in or out which would allow me to have a life of my own. They were isolating me, trying to starve the spirit out of me—waiting for little Jeanne to raise the white flag and throw open the gates for all of them. And then they would pour into my citadel, and they would take my children hostage, kill my soldiers, rape my women, seize anything of value, destroy whatever they couldn't use, and then, when they were thoroughly in control of what little life I had left, *then* they would feed me.

I will tell you a secret. They can't threaten you with starvation, if you learn not to eat. That's right. And that's exactly what I did. I would eat as little as possible, one piece of bread a day. And it worked. My body stayed like the body of a girl. When I died at nineteen, I had still never menstruated. I had found a way to avoid puberty.

I love the body of a young girl. I love my body, my lean body—somewhere between men and women, somewhere where nobody can catch me. I'm a freak. There's a lot of pain in being a freak, but there's a lot of respect. People have to deal with you on your own terms—they can't project their fantasies onto you. There's dignity in being a freak. I was a freak. I still am.

Let me tell you something. There's no such thing as "eating disorders" in a prison camp. There are only eating *strategies*, and mine was very successful. I did not fall into the same trap my mother and my sister did. I did not die by millimeters, as if it were my own fault. If I wasn't getting what I needed to live, I was going to look like it! I was going to make the killers come out and show themselves—and they did.

But I'm getting ahead of myself. My father had a dream about me. I'm sure he had a lot of dreams about me, but this is the only one I ever heard about. In this particular fantasy, or "dream," as he called it, he saw me leaving home to go off with a group of soldiers. And of course, in his infinite masculine wisdom and alcoholic omniscience, he took this to be an omen that I was headed for a life of prostitution. Fascinating interpretation, don't you think, for a man to have about his own daughter? It might have put his mind at ease to know that my military calling was based not on an attraction to men, but on my desire to kill them. Then again, it might not.

In any event, this dream was a real problem for him. You might even say he had become obsessed by it. I mean, he had tried all of the standard remedial methods of battering and calling me a slut, but somehow, in spite of all his efforts, I just couldn't keep myself from reminding him of a prostitute. So, when I was seventeen, my father engaged me to a nice young man. I said I had no intention of marrying him, so the nice young man threatened to take me to court for breach of promise. I said, "Go ahead. It's my father's promise, not mine." He thought he could call my bluff, but I called his. We went to court, and I won. Of course, I made a fool of my father, and after that, life at home was pure hell. And then the enemy soldiers came through Domremy and burned everything they could get their hands on.

So this was a real red letter year for me. The year I was seventeen, my whole family turned against me and the town where I had lived all my life was burned to the ground. But these were just brush fires compared to the real catastrophe. That same year—Hauviette, my best friend—she got engaged. That did it. France's hour of glory had struck. I ran away from home.

One of the hardest parts of running away was leaving my mother. It was like in battle, when the soldier next to you gets his legs blown off by a cannon. You don't want to leave him, but there's nothing you can do for him, and if you stay behind, they'll just get you too. So you leave. Like I left my mother. But it tore my heart out.

The year before I left, she was always telling me to get married, to stop making so much trouble for my father. But way in the back of her eyes—underneath all those layers of wife and mother—I could still see those embers of her trip to Rome smoldering in her memory, like the remains of some sacred fire at the altar of her lost girlhood. I wanted to take those embers and fan them back into flame, and then I wanted to take that flame, and live out my life—not just one or two episodes, but my *whole* life—in the blaze of that hot, bright fire.

I left without telling my mother I was going, but I felt—and I still feel—that I have her blessings. I rode out with the standard of my mother's lost girlhood. I am the champion of lost girlhood dreams!

After I left home, I went to stay with my cousin. His wife was expecting a baby and she needed some help—but I didn't stay long. I talked my cousin into taking me to see the governor of the fort at Vaucouleurs. I wanted this man to give me a military escort to Chinon, where I could see the king.

The first time we went, things didn't go so well. In fact, they didn't go at all. The governor took one look at me, and started laughing. He told my cousin to take me home again, or else he was going to turn his soldiers loose on me. Big joke, right?

So I went back with my cousin. I went back, and I thought about what had happened. And the more I thought, the more I kept seeing this big, red, long, hot, heavy, wool dress—the dress I had been wearing, the dress I always wore—the dress that every other woman in my village had always worn. And the more I thought about this big, red, long, hot, heavy, wool dress—the more I began to see things the same way the governor had.

That dress had a voice. In fact, that dress spoke louder than I did. Before I even opened my mouth, that dress had already introduced me: "Hi. You don't know me, but I'm someone who chooses to wear this thing which is uncomfortable, impractical, and unsafe. I'm someone who chooses to wear this thing that won't let me run, fight, ride a horse, swim—that won't even let me walk outside without falling over, unless I have both hands free to hold up my skirts. Hi. You don't know me, but I'm someone who chooses to wear this thing that will make rape very, very easy for men—even though I know that men will rape any chance they get, and I don't really want that to happen. So, how about it, big boy? Think you can take me seriously wearing this thing *you* wouldn't be caught dead in?

Right. So I went back to see the governor in real clothes, like the clothes men get to wear. And, what a surprise, this time he let me talk.

Now, there are a lot of myths and theories about why this macho governor gave me, a young female nobody, that escort. Some people say I convinced him with a supernatural prophesy. Others say he believed some legend that a woman would save France. Or he was talked into it by other people. And my favorite: He was just desperate enough to try anything.

The truth is, there is no man on earth who can stand in the way of a woman who is utterly convinced of the rightness of her actions.

So why, since we women are usually right, are we still stuck in the Dark Ages? Because we don't *feel* like we're right. Well, if we are, *why* don't we feel like it? Because we're waiting for permission. You will notice that my career began to slide after the king was crowned and I began to need his permission. Before that, nothing could stop me and my voices. But as soon as I started waiting for permission—I lost my timing, I lost my momentum, and finally I lost my confidence.

Anyway, I went to the governor, and the governor gave me the escort, and I went to the king, and the king gave me the army, and I went to Orléans, and I lifted the siege, and I won all my battles, and I took the king to Reims to be crowned, and all of these things happened for the same reason—I was one hundred percent sure I was right.

Which brings me back to that Easter Day at Mélun, the beginning of the end. Like I told you, I was standing on the walls of the city, the crowds were all cheering, the bells were ringing—and then I heard my voices. And my voices told me I would be captured soon.

My voices never lied to me. My father lied, the king lied, the generals lied, the bishops lied. But my voices never lied. One month after Easter, I was captured.

"I was captured." Captured, hell! Like I told you, I was ditched. Let's be honest. I can't even say I was betrayed. That might actually have required some forethought. No, I was ditched.

So, there I was, a prisoner of war. It was May 23, 1430. I was all of eighteen.

For the first few days, I actually believed I would be rescued. I believed the king would send the army to get me. I would sit in my cell and imagine I could hear their trumpets in the distance. That was June. By July, I said to myself, "Well Jeanne, the king is holding back the troops. He is raising your ransom money."

That was July. By August, I said to myself, "Well, Jeanne, they are negotiating. Charles is having trouble getting all that money together. After all, you're not cheap." It never occurred to me that he wouldn't save me—I was the hope and promise of France. I was a national hero. I was even more popular than the king. Of course, he would save me. Right.

So that was August. By November, I knew something was wrong, but I didn't know what. The king was clearly not doing anything, but why? Like a detective, I began looking for clues among the details of my brief, but spectacular career. I thought back a year earlier to the scene at Reims.

Okay. Here it is. It's the inside of the cathedral at Reims, Coronation Day. It's a beautiful July day, and the sun is streaming through the stained glass windows, and the bells are all chiming, and the air is sweet with the smell of incense. And the pews are all full of soldiers, and officers, and counts, and dukes, and knights—and their women, all dressed in satins, and lace, and velvet.

And here are the priests, and the abbots, and the bishops. And the Archbishop of Reims is here, wearing this beautiful robe made out of gold cloth. And here's Charles, standing in the front of the church, dressed like a king, waiting to be crowned according to the ancient traditions handed down by generation after generation of French kings. And here, standing next to him, in the place of highest honor, is a seventeen-year-old peasant girl in full armor. . . . Now, can you tell me what's wrong with this picture?

18

See, what everyone else knew and I didn't, was that I had broken all the rules. Here I was: A peasant, strike one. A child, strike two. And a female, strike three big time. Actually any one of those is an automatic out, but I was all three at the same time. And if that wasn't bad enough, I was also illiterate, outspoken, and dressed like a man! I mean, we're talking about somebody so far out in left field, they're beyond the bleachers! But, all the same, there I was, right up there next to the king.

So in December of 1430, alone in my little prison cell, I began to consider for the first time the people who had been sitting in the pews that day, the people who had followed the rules so carefully. They passed their property and their titles down to their oldest sons, and then they passed their daughters down to somebody else's oldest son. They arranged their whole lives around their real estate—and this was considered high class!

Alone in my prison cell, I also began to consider the high-ranking officers, the ones who were supposed to be driving the English out of France— or, at least that's how I understood it. To them, the army was a career, which explains why we were still fighting the Hundred Years' War. The first rule of promotion is, "Cover your ass." This means make friends in high places, never question authority, and above all, never ever do anything that involves the slightest personal risk.

Alone in my prison cell, I also considered the "men of God," the clergy. They knew the good Lord helps them that help themselves, so that's what they did. They helped themselves to other people's money, to other people's land, and to other people's daughters. The name of the game here was, "Raise the most money in the name of the Lord, keep a low profile, and be able to quote some authority for all your actions, preferably the Bible, but anything in Latin will do."

So here is this cathedral full of people who have devoted their whole lives to playing by the rules, inching their way along, one square at a time—and along comes this peasant girl nobody, this girl nobody who has taken a shortcut right around all their precious titles and bloodlines, and who is right up there next to the king! This peasant girl nobody who has never held any rank at all, but she's riding at the head of the army! This peasant girl nobody who belongs to a church that thinks women are too sinful to be priests, but the angels are talking to her! Obviously, there is something wrong here.

I mean, here they are, these people who have spent their whole lives waiting in line to buy tickets to see God. And they've made up all these elaborate rules to make sure they get the good seats, while everyone else has to take standing room in back. And now, here's this little peasant girl nobody—walking right past the whole line of them, right into the theatre, with no ticket at all!

Now, there's two conclusions they can draw: One, they have wasted their entire lives. Their place in line is meaningless, the reservations made in their name by their ancestors are meaningless, the fact they can afford box seats is meaningless, because you don't need tickets to see God.

And then there's the second conclusion: The girl is wrong. Dead wrong.

In December 1430, on the eve of my nineteenth birthday, alone in my little prison cell, I finally figured out why there hadn't *been* any rescue or ransom and why there was never *going* to be any rescue or ransom. I was the enemy.

So that was December. In January, the Duke of Burgundy turned me over to the church Inquisition. I was no longer a prisoner of war. I was a heretic. A woman who hears voices is a lot more dangerous than a woman with an army. Keep that in mind.

Part II

So . . . how *do* you torture a woman?

Well, you can tie her up on the rack and rip her bones apart from the sockets. That's one way. Or you can tear apart her mind and her body. Now, there's two ways to do this: You can pry her body away from her mind, or you can pry her mind away from her body. Either way, it works out to the same thing. You stop the woman. She can think but not act, or she can act but not think.

To pry her body away from her mind, you need to physically humiliate her. Of course, rape is the most traditional method, but it's not the only one, by any means. You can ridicule her body, or make fun of the things she does. You can make her self-conscious about her looks. You can make her strap her breasts in. You can make her embarrassed about her periods. You can make her frightened of puberty, frightened of sex, frightened of aging, frightened of eating. You can terrorize her with her own body, and then she will torture herself.

Now, if you want to pry her mind apart from her body, you have to make her believe she's crazy. I mean, you can put her in a courtroom and have all the experts certify that she's mentally incompetent, but again—there are a lot of other ways to go about this. You can just annul her. We all know how that goes. Interrupt her, change the subject, ignore her, patronize her, trivialize her, dismiss her. You can deprive her of her history, of her art, of her spiritual traditions. You can restrict her contact with other women. You can have a fit over women-only space—like the whole rest of the world isn't men-only. . . . You can *lie* to her so chronically and so comprehensively, the lying becomes the entire context for her existence. It's really not terribly hard to make a woman believe she's crazy, if you control all the resources.

And if you're a real expert at torture, you can do both at the same time! You can offer to love her body, if she'll just give up her mind. Or you can offer to love her mind, and at the same time reject her body. That's what I got. The Church had so much love for my soul, they just had to burn my body. On the other hand, they promised to take care of my body, if I would give up everything I knew was true.

You think the days of the Inquisition are over? Every woman who's ashamed of her body is a victim of torture. Every woman who doubts her own judgment is a victim of torture. So just how many women do you know who haven't been pulled apart?

Well. My torture. As I say, I got it both ways. In the prison cell, they were after my body. In the courtroom, they were going for my mind.

I was moved to a castle in Rouen for the trial. My cell was dark and cold, and I was never allowed to leave it, except to go to the courtroom. My feet were chained to a wooden beam. It was uncomfortable, but it wasn't all that different from the other places where I had been a prisoner for the last eight months, except for one thing. I wasn't allowed to be attended by women.

In this prison, I had a special detail of guards, five of them, English soldiers. Three in the cell with me and two outside the door, twenty-four hours a day, seven days a week, for five months. They were animals.

They insulted me, they threatened me, they ridiculed me, they degraded me. They never got tired of cruelty. They never gave me one minute of privacy. They polluted every square inch of my cell.

They did everything but rape me, but that wasn't out of any respect for me—oh, no. There were two reasons they didn't. First, I was difficult to get at, because I was wearing men's clothes. I had hose tied to the doublet at twenty points each, and I wore leggings which were tightly laced. And then, my virginity was an issue at the trial—you know, virginity being equated with credibility. So after the court had me examined to certify the presence of my hymen, well, the guards didn't dare do anything after that. Not because it would have been rape. Oh no, not at all. Because it would have been tampering with the evidence.

But rape, of course, is not the issue. The fear of rape, as men have known for years, is just as effective as the real thing. The woman is scared to live alone, scared to go places by herself, scared of the dark, always looking over her shoulder, waking up at the least sound in the middle of the night. She is perpetually distracted, self-conscious, subverted, terrorized. She might just as well have been raped, which of course, is the whole point.

In my little cell in Rouen, surrounded by my five guards, the atmosphere of rape was suffocating. And it had nothing to do with sex. It had to do with degradation. They wanted to make me despise myself. I chose to despise them instead.

Anger is a discipline. I practiced my anger the way some people practice piano. It takes energy to be outraged. It's hard work. Especially when the abuse becomes routine. Some days I was tired and sore and feeling sorry for myself. Some days I just wanted to pretend I didn't hear them. Some days I wanted to pretend I was above it all. But I would always say to myself, "Jeanne, if you don't resist this abuse, then you accept it, and if you accept it, then you deserve it, and if you deserve it, you are a dead woman—and that's exactly what they want!

So no matter how sick, how tired, how weak I was, I would always rise to the occasion, throw back the insult, protest the abuse, and demand my rights as a human being. Of course, this had no effect on them, but it kept me alive.

I want to say something about my experience. I hear a lot of talk about women forgiving men. I don't believe it. I have experienced almost every form of cruelty men can inflict on women, and I am here to tell you that no woman can forgive it or ignore it, and furthermore no woman should ever try. There is no such thing as forgiveness—there is only resolution. With abuse, you either resist it or you accept it, period. Anything else is just fooling yourself.

So I fought for my body in the cell. In the courtroom, I had to fight for my mind.

Let me tell you about my trial. I had two judges, two officers of the court, three notaries, and an usher to escort me back and forth from my cell . . . and thirty-two doctors of theology, sixteen bachelors of theology, four doctors of civil rights, seven men with special licenses, five doctors of canon law, fifteen men with licenses in canon law, seven medical doctors, eleven masters of arts, sixteen assistants and expert witnesses, twenty-three priests, five bishops, three abbots—and a cardinal, in a pear tree. After all, you can't be too careful with these teenage girls.

The trial lasted five months. It focused on two issues—my voices and my clothing. Now, that seemed strange to me at first, because both of those things are so irrelevant. I mean, why would all these important men be so interested in something so personal? I kept trying to skip over their questions or change the subject, but time after time, day after day, they would always come back to those same two things, my voices and my clothes. Of course. My perceptions and my identity. They knew exactly what they were doing. They wanted me to renounce my voices— that is, to invalidate my perceptions, and to wear a dress—that is, to change my identity to suit them. Of course. Haven't we all?

And there was something else they were very interested in. My attempt to escape. Men are always fascinated by women's attempts to escape, but only if we fail. If we succeed, they pretend we don't exist. My attempted escape? I had jumped off the roof of the castle where I had first been held prisoner. This was very interesting to them, because they thought I might have been trying to kill myself. I don't know how they came up with that. The tower was only seventy feet off the ground.

The reason they were so fascinated with this little episode was because trying to kill yourself is considered a sin. What I want to know is why isn't it a sin to make a woman want to kill herself? Probably because that would put the Pope on the "Ten Most Wanted" list. So they kept asking me over and over, "Weren't you trying to kill yourself when you jumped?" And I would always answer, "I was trying to escape." Like there's some difference.

So they didn't get what they wanted, but it didn't matter, because the fact I didn't die from a seventy-foot drop, proved I was a witch anyway. And there, I have to agree with them. Most of us women who survive our own best efforts at self-destruction are pretty miraculous, don't you think?

So on and on it went. Actually for a while, I was holding my own. They'd ask these idiotic questions, like, "Jeanne, do St. Catherine and St. Margaret have . . . ahem . . . hair?" And I'd say, "Hey, you'd better believe it!" Or, "Now, Jeanne . . . hmmm . . . when St. Michael appeared to you, was he . . . hmmm . . . wearing any clothes?" And I'd say, "What do you think? God's too poor to give him any?" Lots of people in the courtroom would crack up. In fact, I think a lot of them were secretly rooting for me.

I think my judge Cauchon knew it too. I was supposed to have two judges, but one of them never showed up. Really, it was Cauchon's baby. He told everybody he wanted to have a "beautiful trial." It was going to be a big boost for him. You see, he was on a career track. He had gone to the University of Paris, and then they sent him to Rome, and then they made him the Bishop of Beauvais, so he was moving right up the old ladder.

But then he rang into a snag with the war, and he had to choose which side to be on. Since all his rich friends in Beauvais were for the English, he decided he was too, which was fine until I came along and the French began to win. Two years before this trial, all his hot-shot friends got kicked out of Beauvais, and he lost his territory. So now this refugee bishop was going to use this trial to stage his big come-back. That's why he invited all these prominent people to see it. And here I was, making a monkey out of him!

Let me tell you something about men. They can't stand to lose face. It's difficult for us women to understand how very, very important this is to men, because we have never been allowed to have enough face to lose. We tend to be more concerned with things like the justice of an issue, or finding a peaceful solution. It's difficult for us to understand how the most important thing, even in the case of war, is to find some way for all the men involved to save face. It would almost be funny how childish they are, except that these children are running the world—and they have almost ruined it.

And these rules of face-saving are hard on women. When a woman challenges a man, it's not enough for him to prove she's wrong. To save face, he has to annihilate her. And this is what Cauchon was out to do.

After my sixth day in court, he moved the trial to my little cell. No more audience. Just him, a few assistants, and the notaries. Things went downhill for me. Without the pressure of the spectators, I couldn't make them skip over the questions anymore. I had to give them what they wanted.

And when it was all over, five months and hundreds of pages later, this is what they came up with. Here are my charges: One, disobeying my parents and causing them anxiety. Two, wearing men's clothes. Three, taking a vow never to have sex with men—can't imagine why. Four, listening to voices on the sole basis they brought me comfort. Five, believing in these voices without the church's permission. Six, refusing to recognize the church's right to judge my actions.

These were my crimes. And if you think they don't burn women for these anymore—ask any dyke! She'll tell you.

So they take me out of my cell. They take me to a cemetery—that's appropriate, isn't it? And there are these two big platforms they've built just for the occasion. This one here's for me, and that one's for the judges. And over there is the little cart with the executioner, waiting to take me to the public square, where the stake is.

And I want you to imagine for a minute, all around you, all over this room, a sea of faces—ignorant, vicious faces. Faces of people who have come to watch you die. Faces that expect it—no, that insist on it! Faces that should be familiar: working class faces, faces from your own neighborhood, faces of old women like your grandmother, faces of little girls like your sisters—human faces. And all of them are completely unrecognizable.

There is not one glimmer of sympathy, not one spark of compassion. They are all looking at you, but they don't see you. They see their long-awaited revenge, they see their promised entertainment, they see their reward for living cowardly and conservative lives. The world owes them your death—and they're going to get it!

I had been in battle before. I had expected to die many times. I had even tried to kill myself. But nothing in my experience had prepared me for this, for these hideous faces. Fear is one thing, but this was horror.

So while they were reading my sentence, I broke down and confessed. I renounced my voices and promised to wear a dress. What happens to women when we finally do break—which is usually after almost superhuman suffering? Do we get a reprieve? Are we released, forgiven?

Does the torture stop, the pressure let up? I have seen all kinds of women give in in all kinds of ways: to harassment, to guilt, to sex, to drugs, to alcohol, to mental illness. And in every single instance—listen to me!—the abuse increases. There is no mercy for women, because our crime is our gender. We have to fight.

So, I confessed. And, like most women, I expected some reward for surrendering myself, for betraying my voices, for denying my purpose, for selling out every single scrap of my integrity. I expected to be moved to a church prison where there would be other women prisoners and women attendants. But that didn't happen. They took me back to my old cell, back to my five guards. Only now I had to wear a dress.

Meanwhile, the crowd with the faces was starting to get ugly. They didn't care anything about heretics, or laws, or procedures, or confessions. All they wanted was to see somebody suffering more than they were. When they realized they had been cheated out of an execution, they were ready to riot. So you see, the political pressure was building to find some way to make me break the terms of my penance.

It was on Thursday when I signed the confession and they took me back to my cell. On Saturday, the guards opened the door and let an Englishman into my cell. He was well-dressed, and I thought he must be a lord or something. I stood up and faced him to see what he wanted. He said my name, "Jeanne?" "Yes?" Wham! "The Maiden?" Wham! And I'm on the floor and he kicks me in the ribs, in the stomach, and I roll into a ball. He's kicking my back and my legs. And then he's on the floor over me, and he's pulling up my dress—with one hand!

If I had been wearing men's clothes, he would have had to use both hands. He would have had to untie forty knots and two sets of lacings—with both hands. I would have made him pay for it, you better believe it. But with a dress? One hand, one movement. That's what dresses are

28

about, isn't it? Accessibility? I don't see where that's changed much in five hundred years. And neither has rape.

So he's got my skirt up, and I'm lying on the floor, and he's smacking my face back and forth. Wham! Wham! Wham! And with his other hand, he's taking out his penis! And here's my precious girl body—my own sweet body—my body, me! It's me! And he's jamming his big, ugly thing into my sweet body! And he's slamming into my body. Wham! Wham! And I can't focus my eyes and my nose is bleeding, and he's talking between his' teeth in some language I can't understand. And then suddenly he's standing up and kicking me again—in the uterus, in the back. And then he's gone. And the guards are standing around, and I think, " Well, they're going to rape me, too"—but they didn't.

You see, it's like a cat playing with a crippled bird, pouncing and shaking it while it struggles to get away—but then, as soon as the bird dies, the cat just drops it and walks away. The game is over. And there I was—raped, battered, broken. The game was over. After five months, it was finally over. Oh, they stood around for a while, hoping I would show some sign of my old spirit, but I didn't—so they just walked off.

That was Saturday. On Sunday morning, I woke up to feel one of the guards taking off my dress. He threw my old clothes at me and told me I could put them on or go naked. Now you have to understand, it was against the terms of my penance ever to wear men's clothes again. I begged him to give me back the dress, but he wouldn't. They just laughed at me and waited. I stayed in bed pleading with them until noon, but then I had to get up and pee, so finally I put on my old clothes again— the "men's" clothes. And of course, the minute I did that, the guards went to report it to Cauchon. And he and the other court officials came scurrying like rats to see for themselves.

And then the miracle happened. I had been raped and battered and broken. I had denied my voices. For three days, I hadn't known who I

29

was. But suddenly when I put on my old clothes again, my "men's" clothes—no!—my *human* clothes—I came back to myself. I knew who I was again, and I was all through with compromise.

Nobody mentioned my swollen and bruised face, and I didn't mention it either. I told them I was wearing men's clothes of my own free will. I looked right at those guards and told them that no one had made me wear them. I said that as long as I had to live in a man's world, I would dress like a man. If they would move me to a decent prison where I could be with other women, I would wear anything they liked.

And then they asked me if I had heard the voices of Catherine and Margaret since Thursday when I confessed. And I told them, "Yes, as a matter of fact, I have. And my voices told me that by trying to save my life, I had condemned myself. My voices told me that every single thing I had ever done in my whole life, I had done well, and it was a lie to say anything different." Of course, the notaries were writing all of this down as fast as they could, and when I got to that last part, they wrote "fatal answer" in the margin.

So that was Sunday. That was when I rose again from the dead. Rape is the crucifixion of women, and I am proof that there is life after rape. Even more life, because when a woman is raped, she buries that part of herself which is accessible to men. Now, in a rape culture, they'll try to make you believe that's everything—but it's not. She rises again with what no man can penetrate, her self-esteem. She is reborn, in her own image.

Wednesday morning they came to get me. I didn't have to measure myself against the world anymore. I was my own person, and I cried uncontrollably. They gave me communion, and then they took me out to the executioner's cart. This priest who used to spy on me in my cell, tried to climb into the cart and get me to forgive him. They pulled him out and told him he better leave town if he knew what was good for

30

him. There were a hundred English soldiers escorting my cart to the market square. This time, they had put the platforms in the same place with the stake. I guess they didn't want to risk another confession.

They put a hat on my head, a hat with names on it. "Idolater, Heretic." And there was a sign on the platform where I stood, "Jeanne—Liar, Seducer."

Someone gave a long sermon. I wasn't listening. This time I didn't even notice the faces that had bothered me so much a week earlier. They hadn't changed, but I had. I had been raped.

They read my sentence. I remember they called me a dog returning to my vomit. And they excommunicated me. I prayed. People were laughing at me. Then I was turned over to the bailiff. Two men shoved me over to the platform with the stake, and they threw me up onto it. The stake was very high, so that everyone could see it. Usually the executioner kills the victim, so they don't actually have to burn to death, but the stake was so high in my case, he couldn't reach me to do his job. I had a little wooden cross inside my clothes, against my bosom. A priest sent to a church in the square for the ceremonial cross, and he held it up so that I could see it. And they tied me to the stake and lit the fire.

Between the time they lit the fire and the time I lost consciousness—was a long time. It was a long time to wonder where God was. The God I had been taught to believe in was no match for my suffering. My voices were still with me. They're always with me, because they're part of me, but where was this loving Father with all the power to save people, or at least to make me die quickly?

Do you remember when Dorothy exposed the Wizard of Oz, and you heard the booming voice say, "Pay no attention to the man behind the curtain"? Well, let me tell you, when we women begin to expose the actions of men, we hear this sacred voice urging us to protect and forgive.

31

This voice is so ancient, so powerful, so authoritative that we're overcome with guilt and shame—even though *we're* the victims!

I'm here today to tell you something about that voice. That voice telling you to protect and forgive men, that voice urging you to be a little more patient, a little more tolerant—that is not the voice of God. It's the voice of the men behind the curtain. The only reason it sounds like God is because they have been amplifying themselves for two thousand years and using a lot of special effects.

Tied to that stake, watching the fire come closer and closer, I realized that God the Father was a lie. He's an invention of the good old boys to cover their tracks and their asses. I realized that the closest I had ever come to any real sense of spirituality was alone with my voices, or in the company of other women.

I realized what a fool I had been to waste my time crowning some man king, as if he had some divine right to rule. I realized what a fool I had been for trusting a church run by men who only worshipped themselves and each other. I realized what a fool I had been to lead one army of men out against another, as if it could make any possible difference which side won. And I realized what a fool I had been to believe I would be saved from the actions of men by a god they had created in their own image.

God the Father was a lie then and is a lie now, and all the hierarchies modeled after him—the governments, the armies, the churches, the corporations, *the families!*—are illegitimate. We will not convert them. They will martyr us. *We will not convert them.* We must fight for our own causes, women's causes. We must clothe ourselves in self-respect, arm ourselves with our finely-tempered rage, and obey only those voices that we women alone can hear.

Epilogue

So. "Saint Joan of Arc." Twenty years later they had a second trial to "rehabilitate" me. You see, I was holding my own as a national hero, and if there's one thing the Church can't stand, it's competition. Besides, the myth of a feminine, simple-minded peasant girl had begun to replace the memory of the cross-dressing butch with the smart mouth.

Well, this second trial was pretty much a formality without the star witness. Everybody knew ahead of time what the outcome would be. Not much interesting, except for one thing. Hauviette—my best friend—she testified. I didn't think she'd even remember me.

I remembered her. Hauviette and I had been very, very close, until the year I ran away. We had grown up together. We had taken our first communion together, which was a very special thing. See, it was a custom in my village for the girls who shared their first communion to sleep with each other. She would come over to my house, or I would go over to hers. We would sleep in the same bed together.

Sometimes we would pretend we were on a very small boat in the ocean, and I had rescued her. I would hold her in my arms, and my heart would be so full of tenderness, it would make me feel light-headed. Or sometimes we would pretend that she had found me wounded in the forest and had taken me to her cottage, where she would bandage my wounds and cover me with kisses.

Hauviette and I were more than best friends. We were one soul. We knew this, and we had always planned to live together after we grew up. But, like I said, there was this terrible thing, puberty.

Hauviette got engaged. I wouldn't even speak to her. How could she do that to me, after I went to so much trouble to break off my engagement?

So I left Domremy. I left, and I didn't tell her I was going. I said good-bye to all my other friends—but not to her.

Anyway, here she is twenty years later, testifying. And what does she say? She says she cried her eyes out when she heard I had left Domremy. She says she loved me because I was so good. And then she called me her lover. She's forty years old and married, standing in front of a room full of Catholic priests and judges, and she says this about a girl who's been dead for twenty years, a girl who left her without saying good-bye.

Hauviette. She had more courage than I did. It was easier for me to face the English army, the French Inquisition, and even the executioner than to face her and say, "I love you." There is one crime I committed. It's one they overlooked in my trial, but it's the one for which I suffered the most—the one for which I suffer every day. I confess it. I denied my love for a woman, and I denied the woman who loved me.

So there was no "Saint Joan of Arc," with her legacy of glorious martyrdom. But there was a Jeanne Romée who made the terrible, terrible mistake of trying to find a substitute in the world of men for the love she had experienced in the arms of a woman.

THE END

The Roar of Silence Trilogy
with the Afterpiece
Battered on Broadway

". . . we should die of that roar which is the other side of silence."
—George Eliot

"You loved a white girl! You loved her for fourteen years! You loved me!" Elizabeth Van Lew (Carolyn Gage) pleads with Mary Bowser (Jolie Johnson) for a "sisterhood" that will not challenge her racism or classism, in *Mason-Dixon*.

Mason-Dixon

A One-Act Play

Cast of Characters

MARY ELIZABETH BOWSER—an African-American woman, age 44.

ELIZABETH VAN LEW—a white woman, age 44.

The action takes place in the parlor of Mary Bowser's home in Philadelphia, one afternoon in late summer, 1861.

MASON-DIXON

The set is a parlor in a house in Philadelphia. The room is furnished simply, but with great care. Part of the parlor has been converted into a schoolroom with a desk, blackboard, and a row of benches. It's 1861, shortly after the battle of Bull Run. MARY ELIZABETH BOWSER, a Black woman who is 44, sits working at her desk. There is a knock on the door. MARY rises and crosses to open it. A white woman, 44, stands in the doorway. She is elegantly dressed. She is ELIZABETH VAN LEW, daughter of the former enslavers of MARY from Virginia. MARY says nothing for a moment. The two women stand looking at each other.

ELIZABETH: [*After a moment, deeply moved by the reunion*] Elizabeth.

MARY: I'm sorry but there's no one here by that name.

ELIZABETH: Elizabeth Bowser.

MARY: You are mistaken. My name is Mary.

ELIZABETH: Don't you recognize me?

MARY: [*After a moment*] No.

ELIZABETH: Elizabeth Van Lew. From Richmond.

MARY: I'm sorry, but I have never been to Richmond. You have mistaken me for someone else. [*She closes the door. She crosses back to the desk, sits, and begins to work again. Agitated, she is unable to read. She crosses to the window and stands to one side of the curtain, peeking out to the street. There is a soft knock at the door again. She backs away from it, looking at it.*] Who's there?

ELIZABETH: [*Through the door*] Elizabeth.

MARY: There's no one here by that name.

ELIZABETH: [*Through the door*] It's *my* name.

MARY: [*After a moment of indecision*] NO! [*There is silence, and then another knock. MARY ignores it. She returns to the desk. The knock comes again. This time MARY springs up, rushes to the door and throws it open.*] No, no, no, no, no! [*ELIZABETH stands waiting.*] The woman you are looking for is dead. [*ELIZABETH says nothing.*] What do you want?

ELIZABETH: May I come in?

MARY: No. No, no, no, no.

ELIZABETH: What can I do?

MARY: Go away.

ELIZABETH: I can't. [*The two women stand there deadlocked.*]

MARY: I can't let you in.

ELIZABETH: Could we go someplace else?

MARY: No.

ELIZABETH: Elizabeth . . .

MARY: Elizabeth is dead.

ELIZABETH: [*Angry*] Many people are dead. Many more people are going to die. May I come in?

MARY: You don't like to ask do you? You just can't stand to hear "no" from a Negro, can you?

ELIZABETH: I can't stand to hear "no" from anyone. [*She enters the room and turns to look at MARY.*]

MARY: [*Very quietly*] Get out.

ELIZABETH: No. [*Mary glares at her.*] You don't like to hear it either. You should never have opened the door a second time. It's your fault I came in. If you don't want a thing to happen, you don't allow it to happen.

MARY: I told you to go away.

ELIZABETH: If you don't want a thing to happen, you don't *allow* it to happen. It's a question of resolution. [*She takes off her gloves and sits.*] As I said, many people are dying. No doubt you are following the war with some interest.

MARY: The war does not interest me.

ELIZABETH: It interests me. [*She takes out her watch.*] General Ben Butler interests me, also. He gave me something to put in my watch. [*She takes out a folded piece of paper and hands it to MARY.*] It's a code. I keep it on my body at all times, in the back of my watch case. Were anyone in Richmond to find out about this little scrap of paper in the back of my watch, I would be placed in Libby Prison and then hanged. Were anyone interested in seeing me dead, they would only have to send a letter to anyone in the Confederacy saying, "Look in Miss Van Lew's watch case." The letter would not even have to be signed. It would be that simple. As I say, many people are dying.

MARY: Your watch does not interest me. [*She hands back the paper.*]

ELIZABETH: Well, that's a relief.

MARY: If you were on fire, I wouldn't spit on you to put it out, but that doesn't mean I'd take the trouble to set the match. Miss Van Lew, you make no impression on me at all. Like a footprint in the creek bed, you are gone as soon as you're here. You just stir up a little mud, and then you are gone, and that creek flows on just as cold and as fast as it did before you stepped in it. And when you leave this room, you won't even have been here. You may dent my chair for this little minute, but then it's going to puff up again, and won't even carry the memory you ever sat in it. That chair and this room and myself, we will forget that you ever came here, because you are so slight, you've never been where you've gone. And whatever you came here for, looking me up after thirty years, you might just as well leave now, because when you open your mouth, it's just wind through the leaves to me. I am a free woman, and I've been free twice as long as I was your slave.

ELIZABETH: And who gave you that freedom?

MARY: [*Defensive*] Me. Myself. I gave myself my freedom. And I give myself my freedom every day. I give myself right now the freedom not to remember Richmond, or Church Hill, or Miss Elizabeth Van Lew.

ELIZABETH: That's freedom—not being allowed to think?

MARY: The South is not thinking! The South is dreaming one big nightmare. I was asleep and dreamt I was in hell. And then I woke up here in Philadelphia and I can't be bothered with dreams anymore. They are nothing to me. Nothing to me! Just like you.

ELIZABETH: [*Looking at the room*] You support yourself.

MARY: God loves me so much I get the rent free.

ELIZABETH: What do you do?

MARY: I teach. I teach Negro children. They hang people for doing that where you come from. It's easy to die in the South. Maybe that's why your watch doesn't interest me.

ELIZABETH: I taught you.

MARY: No ma'am, you didn't. I learned what I learned by myself.

ELIZABETH: [*Losing her temper*] If you will give yourself permission to remember, you and I used to climb up in that secret room over the portico and I would go over my lessons with you.

MARY: I don't remember.

ELIZABETH: Yes, you do. You couldn't forget that room. There isn't another room like that anywhere in the world. We had to crawl through a trap door in the ceiling to get up to it. One of us had to stand on the other's shoulders, and then she would pull the other one up. You remember it. Just like you remember how I would go over my lessons with you, and how we did that every single day until I turned fourteen and they sent me away to boarding school. I taught you everything.

MARY: I learned from watching and listening. And if some lonesome little white girl wanted to get her Jesus go-to-heaven points by showing her books to a slave—well, I watched and I listened to that too, but you didn't teach me. You white folks have got nothing to teach to us colored people.

ELIZABETH: Well, I believe I'll go now. [*MARY, rigid, watches her.*] You're right. The woman I came to see is not here.

MARY: No former slaves in this house.

ELIZABETH: That's right. Only current ones. [*She crosses to the door.*]

MARY: [*Rising from her desk at this challenge*] You can't play with a grown woman the way you played with a child.

ELIZABETH: I thought you didn't remember.

MARY: I remember. I remember how you always said we were sisters. [*She laughs.*] Your family bought me when I was a baby. They bought me and gave me to you, because we were the same age. Gave me to you like a pony or a dog. And you thought I was your sister!

ELIZABETH: I still think of you as a sister.

MARY: Well, if I sat up on the big hill in the big white house, I guess I could think the whole world was my brothers and sisters, too. But the "brothers and sisters" with the black skin, see, we're not so eager to claim you white folks for kin. We'd rather see you dead.

ELIZABETH: Then you have the perfect opportunity. Write to President Davis and tell him about my watch. I promise I will continue to wear it. But it's obvious I'm wasting my time here. Excuse me. [*She crosses around MARY to the door, then stops.*] By the way, Papa died. [*MARY turns away quickly. ELIZABETH watches her, and then starts to exit.*]

MARY: [*Without looking at her*] Wait.

ELIZABETH: What did you say?

MARY: I said, "Wait." [*ELIZABETH waits.*] I got some things I want to tell you about your papa. [*MARY turns to face her, and ELIZABETH comes back into the room and sits.*] Remember how he let me have my own room in the big house when I was just a little thing. And everybody was saying how fine and generous that was. Fine nothing. He just wanted me where he could get to me easy. And all those nice clothes he bought me, everyone saying it was because you were so fond of me. It was because he liked to look at me. Liked his little pickaninny all dressed up in lace and crinoline. It was all for him. And me, a little girl sold away from her family, living in the big house away from the other slaves, waking up at night, and here's this big white man with the horses and the books and all the fields, the white man with all the big smiles and the soft voice and the candy for the little colored girl, and he's wanting to wrap his body around the little colored child with no mama and daddy. Your papa was bringing me candy and asking me not to tell, and saying one day I was going to have a big house all to myself, and my own slaves. Telling a little colored child she was going to have slaves! Telling me how he loved his slaves, that he wasn't like the rest of the white men. Him telling me he loved me and that doing this was going to prove it. And he'd always say, "Don't tell Elizabeth, because I don't want her to know I love you more than her." And then, that year when you turned fourteen and they sent you to Philadelphia for school—that year he started coming to me every night. Every night while you were gone. And then in the daytime, it was "Yes sir, Mr. Van Lew. That's right Mr. Van Lew." [*She looks at her.*] You think I'm lying about your papa. Your papa who got up and read the Scriptures in the church, your papa who was so good he freed all his slaves. Your papa you thought was sitting right up there between Jesus and God. Your papa was climbing on top of a little colored child all those years. [*ELIZABETH looks down.*] You want to know why we're not sisters? That's why we're not sisters. [*ELIZABETH puts her face in her hands.*] Don't cry for me. That girl is dead. Your papa never touched one bone in this woman's body.

ELIZABETH: Elizabeth—

MARY: My name is Mary.

ELIZABETH: Mary, I—

MARY: Don't say anything. There's nothing you have to say that I want to hear. You and your papa, both of you just loving the "niggers." Loving us to death. [*She rises.*] Get out of my house.

ELIZABETH: You weren't the only one.

MARY: Oh, I have no doubts about that. I'm sure he stuck his thing in every little colored girl he could get his hands on.

ELIZABETH: Not just colored ones. [*MARY is stunned. After a moment, she sits.*] I'm sure Mama guessed. That's why she sent me away to boarding school. I had started to bleed. At school we talked about things that weren't considered proper at home. I started to understand that this special little secret between fathers and daughters was rape. I caught pneumonia that winter and I thought I was going to die. Everyone thought I would die. Do you know why I didn't? Because of you. Because I realized he was doing it to you. I decided to live. I sent him a letter while I was still recovering. I told him that I understood what he had been doing to me and that I was prepared to tell everyone in the county unless he agreed to my conditions. He wrote back such a formal letter. [*She laughs again.*] "I am interested in the details of your proposals." Like a business letter! I had three: Free our slaves, send you to school in Philadelphia, and give me a pistol. He did what I said. When I came home, the slaves were gone, you were in Philadelphia, and I could sleep with a gun under my pillow at night. I never spoke another word to him. We spent thirty years in the same house, and I never spoke another syllable to him.

MARY: That man was the devil.

ELIZABETH: [*Breaking the silence*] Why didn't you write?

MARY: Nothing to say.

ELIZABETH: Why didn't you answer my letters?

MARY: I was hurt. I figured that while you were away at that fancy school, you were beginning to be ashamed of having me for a best friend. I figured you were fixing on taking your place in society and you would be uncomfortable about having me around to watch. I've seen it happen a lot with white children, children who grew up playing together like twins—and then suddenly one day they just stop. Like that. Time for both of them to learn their places. I figured that time had come for you and you were just trying to make it easier, getting me out of the way before you came home a young lady.

46

ELIZABETH: I loved you so much. It broke my heart.

MARY: [*After a minute*] Broke mine too. [*The years of silence rise up like a wall between them.*]

ELIZABETH: Well . . . [*Looking around the room*] It looks like you've got a good income. [*MARY says nothing.*] I didn't come here to talk about the past. I came here for a specific reason.

MARY: Something to do with your watch.

ELIZABETH: That's right. I'm a special agent for the Union army. I have access to the Federal prisons, and I visit the men every week. They keep me informed of troop strengths and movements. I entertain officers in the Confederate army, and get them a little careless with wine and flattery, and they tell me what I want to know, but I don't have access to the information I really need. [*MARY just looks at her.*] This is where you can help me.

MARY: I don't remember saying I was interested in helping you.

ELIZABETH: Helping the Union. Helping your people who are still slaves.

MARY: I have my own way of helping.

ELIZABETH: [*Leaning forward*] You could save thousands of Negro lives. You could be personally responsible for ending the war. [*MARY says nothing.*] You could get me the information about all the rebel plans before their own generals get them.

MARY: And how would I do that?

ELIZABETH: [*She removes a packet of letters from her bag.*] See these letters? These are letters of reference. I can get you a position in the Confederate White House.

MARY: [*In disbelief*] What?

ELIZABETH: I can get you a position as a maid for Jefferson Davis.

MARY: [*Throwing the letters on the floor as if they burned her fingers*] I cannot believe this. I cannot believe that you have come five hundred miles after thirty years to sit in my house and tell me that I have the chance to lick the boots of the man who is the defender of slavery. I cannot believe that you have come here to tell me that I have a chance to go back to the South, to that land of living hell, and watch my people bought and sold on the auction block, whipped like mules, worked 'til they drop in the fields, bred like animals, and hung for looking over their shoulders. I cannot believe that you have come here to look me in the face and tell me that.

ELIZABETH: I would do it myself if I could.

MARY: That's easy to say when you have white skin.

ELIZABETH: Elizabeth—

MARY: Don't call me that slave name!

ELIZABETH: That's my name too.

MARY: That's why they gave it to me. It's a slave name. My name is Mary.

ELIZABETH: Mary. [*A beat*] I am risking my life every day with the work I do. I take books into the prisons for the men, books with pinholes punched over certain letters to spell out a code. Right now, as we talk, there are men digging their way out of Libby prison, tunneling right under it. And when they escape, I will hide them in that same secret room where you and I used to study. I am in as much danger as I ask you to be.

MARY: It's not the danger I'm talking about. I am talking about the degradation. I am talking about setting out the silverware that was paid for with a dozen colored people's lives. I am talking about doing the dirty laundry for some white man who never lifted his finger a day in his life except to beat a colored woman and rape her daughter. I am talking about being ordered around by people who don't bother to learn your name, people who talk right in front of you as if you weren't even there—

ELIZABETH: [*Interrupting*] Exactly! You would stand behind Jefferson Davis at every meal. Like a statue. A statue with ears. You would dust around his desk, set out his mail, burn his discarded papers in the fireplace. You would know everything he planned before it was executed. Do you understand that this information could end the war in six months?

MARY: No.

ELIZABETH: I'm not asking you to do anything I wouldn't do.

MARY: You can't even imagine what it's like to have black skin.

ELIZABETH: I can imagine what it's like to be somebody's property. I know what it's like to be owned and used, just like you do.

MARY: Not just like! You open your mouth to speak, and it may be a woman's mouth, but it's a rich white woman's mouth, and the "rich white" part gets heard loud and clear. I open my mouth and it's nothing. You get hurt by a white man, you can find some other white men to take up your cause. A colored woman gets hurt by a white man, and all the white men are going to look the other way. Don't come up here trading on this sister stuff, because that was nothing but two children who didn't know any better.

ELIZABETH: We *are* sisters, because we have the same enemy.

MARY: My enemy is the white race.

ELIZABETH: Your enemy is the white *man*. And he's my enemy too.

MARY: No, no, no, no, Miss Van Lew. You got that wrong. Your enemy is your own self. You love the white man. When he didn't give you the keys to the kingdom the way you thought he was supposed to, then you found out that by setting yourself up to hate him, you were going to force him to give you those keys anyway. But the one thing you never did was try to find some other way in without the white man's keys. I am not interested in fighting for or against the white man. I can see why, as a white woman you want to try to save him by fighting him. But I don't even give him a thought. These last thirty years while you closed yourself up in that house on Church Hill trying to punish your daddy, these same thirty years I've been working here in Philadelphia, setting up my school, teaching these colored children how to read, how to write, how to understand that history is not what the white folks say it is. I am teaching them how to make a Negro world, so that they won't have to live in a white one. I don't have time to fight the white man. I am too busy creating another world here.

ELIZABETH: A world that many of your people will never live to see.

MARY: I can't change that.

ELIZABETH: Yes, you can. And every time you read about this war, from now on, you will know that you could have done something to stop it, and you didn't. [*She rises to leave.*]

MARY: Miss Van Lew, let me ask you something. [*She turns.*] Do you really think the white folks in the North are going to be any better than the ones in the South?

ELIZABETH: They are against slavery.

MARY: No. They are against the use of slaves in the cotton field as free labor. If cotton grew north of the Mason-Dixon, these Union boys and Mr. Lincoln would sing a different tune, and I guarantee it would sound a lot like "Dixie."

ELIZABETH: I don't believe that.

MARY: Only two reasons the white folks ever do anything for colored people . . . money and fear.

ELIZABETH: Is that why I am working for the Union—for money? Or is it fear?

MARY: You're afraid of losing your life.

ELIZABETH: If I was afraid of that, I certainly wouldn't be an agent.

MARY: Oh, yes you would. You are forty-four years old, and you are afraid you've never lived. You're afraid you never will. You thought you could get your life back by hating your daddy enough, but he's dead now and you still haven't gotten it back. So along comes this war, and you think by joining up with the Union army you can make yourself the enemy of every white man who reminds you of your daddy. You think you can kill them now, and their lives are going to give you back yours. But, see, this is where the white man's got you. You're not going to have your own life until you let go of him. As long as he's making you love him or making you hate him, he's got you.

ELIZABETH: He's got all of us. You just have a little corner of the world that you think is yours, so you call yourself free. You're right. The white man's not going to bother you here. Pay the rent, and he won't come calling. He may even do some repairs. Teach your Negroes all you want. If they want to read books during their break at the factory, who's that going to hurt? Your "freedom" is not something you have won. It's the name of your new prison cell. My cell is even bigger and better furnished than yours, but I have more imagination than you. I know it's a cell. [*A pause*] Let me ask you something. Do you really believe Negro men, when they get a little taste of privilege, are going to treat women any better than white men?

MARY: Of course. We have shared slavery together.

51

ELIZABETH: Look around you! Look at the families you know here in Philadelphia! How often do your so-called free men remember that their wives and mothers and daughters have shared slavery with them?

MARY: [*Defensive*] When we have our own history and our own culture, it won't be like that.

ELIZABETH: You are wrong about that. Gender runs deeper than race. That's something my papa taught me. There is never going to be a Mason-Dixon line for women.

MARY: [*After a moment*] I am not willing to give up my life here to fight a white folks' war. [*ELIZABETH looks at her for a long time.*]

ELIZABETH: You think I'm pathetic, don't you? Don't you? You've gone out in the world and done something with your life, while I shut myself up and hid from it. That's what you think, isn't it? [*MARY says nothing.*] If I weren't white, you'd even feel sorry for me, wouldn't you? [*ELIZABETH laughs.*] Well, here's the funny thing—I feel sorry for you. [*Looking at the papers on MARY's desk*] What are you teaching your children?

MARY: I'm teaching them their own history.

ELIZABETH: Now that's the funny part. You're teaching them to reclaim their history all the time you're running away from yours.

MARY: No.

ELIZABETH: [*Losing control*] Yes! You loved a white girl, Mary Elizabeth Bowser! You loved a white girl! You loved her for fourteen years! You loved me!

MARY: I was too young to know better.

ELIZABETH: You knew better than you do now! Do you want to know why I spent the last thirty years in Church Hill? It wasn't to be

52

near Papa, believe me. It was to guard my freedom. Do you know what my idea of freedom is? You're going to have a good laugh at this—My idea of freedom is a secret room with no windows and a trap door you have to climb up to get into. My idea of freedom is a place no one knew about where I could, for a few hours a day, be somebody not white, not Black, not rich, not poor, not owner, not slave, not southern, not northern, not child, not adult, not female, not male—a place where I could just be myself, and where I could love another person who was just being herself. That was the closest I've ever come to perfect freedom, Mary—that little attic. And that's why I've stayed in that house for thirty years. The thing you have spent your life trying to forget is the only thing in my life which was worth living for. [*She begins to cry, losing control rapidly.*] I have never loved or been loved like that since then, and I will be a dead woman on the day that I let myself forget that love. [*She fumbles for her gloves.*] I'm leaving. Don't worry. I won't bother you again. [*MARY rises.*] No, no—I can see myself out.

MARY: Elizabeth!

ELIZABETH opens the door and exits quickly, on the verge of completely breaking down. She closes the door behind her before MARY can get to it. MARY hesitates with her hand on the door. She freezes for a moment, then turns and looks at the letters scattered on the floor. After a minute, she walks deliberately over to them and picks them up.

THE END

"I'd advise you not to turn your back on me. That's a mistake you won't get to make twice."
Caught trespassing, Kathleen (Wyrda) warns Jane Addams of her dangerous reputation
in *Jane Addams and the Devil Baby*.

Jane Addams and the Devil Baby
A One-Act Play

Cast of Characters

JANE ADDAMS—A woman in her fifties.
MARY ROZET SMITH—Jane Addams' partner.
KATHLEEN—A woman in her seventies.

The play takes place in the parlor of Hull House, Chicago, 1912.

JANE ADDAMS AND THE DEVIL BABY

The scene takes place in the parlor of Hull House, in Chicago in 1912. The parlor is a large room, graciously furnished. There are many works of fine art on the walls. A large window opens into the room. As the play opens, JANE ADDAMS is seated at a desk, trying to answer letters. JANE is fifty-two. A bell is heard offstage, and then MARY ROZET SMITH's voice.

MARY: [*Offstage*] No. [*A pause*] No. It's not here. [*Another pause*] No we didn't hide it. It's never been here. There's no such thing. [*Pause*] No. No. You can't come in and look. No. I'm sorry. [*JANE gets up and crosses to the window.*] No, it's not a question of money. You couldn't see it for five dollars, you couldn't see it for ten dollars, because it's not here. It doesn't exist. Good-bye. [*Another long pause and the bell rings again.*] What? No, you can't see it for twenty! [*The door slams and MARY enters the room. She is a well-dressed woman.*]

JANE: You should have taken the money. Hull House can always use it.

MARY: Oh, I can see the headlines now: "Jane Addams Swindles Chicago Poor In Devil Baby Racket." I'm glad you have a sense of humor about it.

JANE: I don't have much choice.

MARY: I'm tempted to tell them that it's been moved to Milwaukee. They'd sooner travel to Wisconsin than believe me when I tell them it doesn't exist.

JANE: Look. Look out the window.

MARY: [*She crosses to the window. Jane puts her arm around her.*] I don't believe it! The streetcars are backed up for ten blocks!

JANE: Pilgrims.

MARY: Why do they keep coming? We've turned everybody away. Nobody's even gotten into the house. The newspapers have reported that it's nothing but a rumor. But still they keep coming. This is the third week and there are more people every day. The doorbell rings every five minutes. And they're all so sure it's here. They can even describe it to me: the pointed ears, the tail, the cloven hoofs. They tell me their sister-in-law has seen it, or their mother, or the woman who works next to them on the line. They're so sure it's here. Why?

JANE: That's the question. Why? And they're almost all women. Some of them must be losing wages to take time off from work. They seem to be willing to pay almost any price to see it.

MARY: Yesterday a woman came and offered me her life savings if I would show it to her.

JANE: [*Crossing back to her desk*] Why is it so important for them to see it?

MARY: Because they're ignorant and superstitious.

JANE: I think it goes deeper than that.

MARY: Well, I don't. They're coming here the same way they would walk three miles to look at a tenement that collapsed or a fire, or a cart

58

overturned on the street. It's just some kind of freak show for them. Anything morbid to stimulate their curiosity.

JANE: No, I don't agree with you, Mary. I've been at Hull House for twenty years, and every time I attributed something to ignorance or superstition, I was always wrong.

MARY: Don't tell me you believe there's such a thing as the Devil Baby?

JANE: Well, Mary, take a look. [*She gestures towards the window.*] If we don't, we're certainly outnumbered.

MARY: You can't be serious.

JANE: I am.

MARY: Do you mean to tell me that you believe the story that a husband came home drunk one night, tore a holy picture off the wall, told his pregnant wife that he would rather have a devil in the house than a baby, and because of that, her baby turns out to be some incarnation of the devil—horns, hooves, and all? Are you saying that's what you believe?

JANE: I believe there are many ways to see the world, Mary, and those women lined up out there are seeing something—or want to see something—that you and I don't understand. Look at them. They're Italian, Russian, Polish, Irish, Jewish, German. Some of them haven't left their neighborhoods in forty years. Look at them. They're coming on streetcars, on foot, on canes, in wheelchairs. Most of these women have never had a vacation in their lives. But here they are, streaming to Hull House to see this famous Devil Baby they're so sure we're hiding. These women are not tourists. No, they're making some kind of pilgrimage. But why? What is it about this Devil Baby that arouses such a passion in them? [*Just then the sound of the bell is heard, ringing insistently.*]

JANE: I'll go.

MARY: No, I'll go. You try to get some work done. At least something around here will be normal. [*The women kiss on the mouth, affectionately. She exits.*]

JANE returns to her desk and picks up her papers. As she works, the window begins to open very slowly. An elderly woman dressed like a bag lady, crawls in through the window. The woman, KATHLEEN, is an Irish immigrant. She is in poor physical condition, but she is possessed of an unquenchable vitality of spirit. A lifetime of living by her wits has sharpened her perceptions and given her an uncanny ability to read character. JANE has her back towards her and doesn't see her. The woman makes a quick inspection of the room and then begins to creep towards the hall door. JANE notices her. She rises from her desk and begins to follow the woman. The woman reaches the door and begins to turn the knob very slowly. The door fails to open.

JANE: You have to lift the latch while you turn the knob.

KATHLEEN: [*With a thick Irish accent*] That's kind of you to tell me. [*She starts to lift the latch, and then realizes she has been discovered. She whirls around to face JANE.*] Oh! Well, there you are. Why didn't you answer the door? Well, now, I've gone and saved you the trouble of letting me in. [*She pauses.*] I tried the door first, of course. [*She laughs.*] You don't think I'd be climbing in through a window like some kind of heathen, if I hadn't tried the door first? You must have been too busy with your work to hear me knocking.

JANE: We have a bell.

KATHLEEN: Oh, do you now? And I'm a liar, aren't I? And a thief too, no doubt. Well, why don't you just call for the police now, and have old Kathleen arrested for breaking into your house. I'm dangerous, you know. They call me the Butcher of Halsted Street. I'm known to crawl through the windows of rich ladies and slit their throats while they're sleeping in their beds. I'd advise you not to turn your back on me. That's a mistake you won't get to make twice.

JANE: [*Smiling*] What are you doing here?

KATHLEEN: Why, I'm here to murder you and take all your money, I just told you. [*JANE laughs.*] And just what's so funny about that? No, I'll tell you. I can see what you're thinking. I can see what people are thinking, just as clear as you can see those pictures on the wall. It's a second sense I've got. My mother had it too. You're thinking I'm a fine one to be talking murder when I'm standing here with one foot and four toes in my own grave. You see, I know what people are thinking.

JANE: I think you haven't told me why you're here.

KATHLEEN: [*Ignoring JANE's remark*] But I want to tell you you're wrong. If you see an old lady when you look at me, it's no accident. It's taken me years and years to look this old . . . me whole life in fact. Why when I was young, I couldn't have looked this old if me life depended on it. No, it's not an easy thing to be this old, and if I'd had a mind to die, I would have done it years ago before I'd had to work this hard to stay alive. After all this, you think I'm going to let the bastards get me?

JANE: Are you here to see the Devil Baby?

KATHLEEN: Is it here?

JANE: I was asking the question.

KATHLEEN: So was I. Where is it?

JANE: Why do you want to see it?

KATHLEEN: I didn't say I wanted to see it, now did I?

JANE: No, you didn't.

KATHLEEN: Well, now. So don't go thinking you know what I'm thinking. Unless you have the second sight.

JANE: No, I don't have it, unfortunately. Well, since you're not here to see the Devil Baby, and you can't slit my throat unless I turn my back on you, which I'm not going to do, then I guess you'll just have to show yourself back out the window. [*JANE crosses back to her desk and goes back to work. KATHLEEN is agitated.*]

KATHLEEN: [*After a moment of indecision*] Well, now, supposing I *was* here to see the Devil Baby. [*JANE looks up.*] I'm not saying I am. Just supposing. How much are you charging people to see it?

JANE: I haven't said it was here, have I?

KATHLEEN: I'll tell you what, Miss Addams—you are Jane Addams, aren't you?

JANE: Second sight.

KATHLEEN: Well, Miss Addams, I'll strike a bargain with you. [*JANE looks attentive.*] I can see what you're thinking again. You're thinking what does this poor old woman have that she thinks I'm going to want. Now, am I right that's what you're thinking?

JANE: You tell me.

KATHLEEN: I just did. But I'm a business woman too, you see, and I am going to make you an offer that no one else in Chicago is going to match. [*She pauses dramatically.*] If you show me the Devil Baby, I'll bring five hundred women to Hull House to see it, at one dollar a head. That's five hundred dollars for showing me the Baby. [*She says the following with pride.*] Now . . . I don't know what you're charging to see it, but I'm bound to say it to you—that's the best offer you'll get.

JANE: How are you going to bring these five hundred women?

KATHLEEN: That's my secret.

JANE: How do I know they wouldn't come anyway?

KATHLEEN: Oh, you'll know.

JANE: How?

KATHLEEN: Because the women I'll be bringing aren't like any others.

JANE: Who are they?

KATHLEEN: That's my secret.

JANE: I don't see how I can make this deal with you unless you tell me.

KATHLEEN: Five hundred dollars. A woman could help a lot of poor people with five hundred dollars.

JANE: If she knew where it was coming from.

KATHLEEN: You'll have to take my word. Five hundred dollars, take it or leave it. That's a final offer. [*JANE shrugs and goes back to work. KATHLEEN heads for the window. She climbs halfway out, but when she sees that JANE isn't looking, she turns and comes back in the room.*] They're invisible.

JANE: [*Looking up*] What did you say?

KATHLEEN: [*Impatient*] The women. The five hundred women. They're invisible.

JANE: I see.

KATHLEEN: No, you don't. You don't see much. But I do, and that's why if you let me see the Devil Baby, I can bring you these five hundred women.

JANE: Who are invisible.

KATHLEEN: That's right.

JANE: Is the money invisible too?

KATHLEEN: [*Angry at being patronized*] Money's not invisible! [*She walks away shaking her head in disgust.*] "Is the money invisible?" When did you ever see money that was invisible? You could put an old woman's body out on the sidewalk, and just watch the people walk around her like she was a pile of old rags. But just lay two pennies over the poor women's eyelids, and see how long they stay there. "Is the money invisible?" Let me ask you something, Miss Addams—have you ever been poor?

JANE: No.

KATHLEEN: [*KATHLEEN snorts with satisfaction.*] Then half the world's a mystery to you.

JANE: That may be true. [*JANE rises.*] Kathleen, your five hundred women are old and poor, aren't they? They're women that are in the poor house, aren't they?

KATHLEEN: They'll pay a dollar, if that's what you're worried about. I give you my word.

JANE: But they're poor.

KATHLEEN: They're poor, but they'll pay.

JANE: What is it about this Devil Baby that makes a woman who can't even afford the wood to heat her room willing to come to Hull House and offer a life's savings to see it? What is it about this baby with the horns and the hooves that makes them so desperate to come?

KATHLEEN: [*A gleam in her eye*] Show me the baby, and you'll have five hundred chances to ask that question.

JANE: I can't.

KATHLEEN: What do you mean, you can't?

JANE: I can't show it to you.

KATHLEEN: It's the money.

JANE: No.

KATHLEEN: How much do you want?

JANE: It isn't the money. I can't show it to you, because it isn't here.

KATHLEEN: You've hidden it.

JANE: No. It isn't here.

KATHLEEN: You've moved it.

JANE: No. There's no such thing. It doesn't exist.

KATHLEEN: Now I know you're lying. [*She pulls out a knife and holds it to JANE's throat.*] There is a Devil Baby and you'll show it to me!

JANE: [*Surveying her calmly*] No.

KATHLEEN: The games are over, Miss Addams. There is a Devil Baby, I know, because my great-great grandmother saw one, and she told my mother. There was a man in her village whose wife had given birth seven time to little girls, and he cursed her eighth pregnancy, saying he'd as soon have a devil in his house as another girl, and she birthed a Devil Baby. And my great-great grandmother was there at the christening, when they unwrapped the baby and it started to curse, and jumped down and chased the priest all over the church. Don't tell me there's no Devil Baby, when my own great-great grandmother has seen it!

JANE: You can look for yourself.

KATHLEEN: Oh, and wouldn't that be a fine thing—and while I'm off on a goose chase, you call the police on old Kathleen. No, Miss Addams, you and me are going to see that infernal baby together, or not at all. Get up.

JANE: It's not here. [*KATHLEEN looks at her.*] It's not here.

KATHLEEN: [*She looks doubtful for a moment, and then rallies.*] You're lying.

JANE: No, I don't lie, Kathleen, and if I did, I would tell you the Devil Baby is here in Hull House, but it isn't. [*KATHLEEN sits.*] Put the knife on the table. [*KATHLEEN looks at her.*]

KATHLEEN: There's no Devil Baby at Hull House.

JANE: No. [*KATHLEEN puts the knife on the table and begins to cry. JANE puts the knife in a drawer and watches her.*]

KATHLEEN: The bastards! They've got everything! They've got everything! The bastards . . . they've got everything. [*JANE reaches her hand out to KATHLEEN's shoulder.*] Seventy-eight years. Seventy-eight. And they've got everything. Everything. [*KATHLEEN sobs some more, and then she becomes quieter. She looks at JANE.*] There's never been a Devil Baby, has there?

JANE: No.

KATHLEEN: [*Nodding*] Ah. Those clever bastards. They've gone and got away with everything. [*She smiles at JANE.*] Do you know what I live for? Just once—just once to see them get what's coming to them. And I thought with the Devil Baby, it was finally going to be their turn. But, of course . . . nothing again. Me climbing out the window of the poor house, having to beg a ride on the streetcar, and then having to beg the driver to help me up and down, and me with no fare! And all for nothing, again. Those bastards. I bet you it was them that started the rumor in the first place. That would be perfect.

JANE: I don't understand. What would be perfect?

KATHLEEN: The joke. The perfect joke. That a poor woman, married off at thirteen to some drunken shiftless pig who used her like a piece of filth for thirty years and kept her having babies half her life while he's drinking up the money—and her not even being able to take her own children or keep her own wages—and every night him swearing and striking at her and the little ones—and all these years her praying on her knees for the soul of her husband and the life of her babies and the strength to get up in the morning—and what's to show for it, I ask you? The babies, they die anyway, and the ones that don't, they grown up as good as dead. The girls taking to living on the streets, and the boys getting themselves taken off to jail, and in the end, the husband drinking himself to death. And now her, too old and too poor to start over. A lifetime of work and a body half dead with carrying and nursing babies. Now, I ask you, where did all those prayers go? Up the chimney like smoke? And there's not even a Devil Baby to show for it.

JANE: So the Devil Baby is an answer to prayer?

KATHLEEN: To see just once in the flesh—for all the world—*in the flesh!*—the living incarnation of the father's sins visited on the children. Oh, a dozen times I could have birthed that devil. I have. I have! A son who steals from his own mother. Who takes the bottle just like his father? Who comes after his own sisters like he was some kind of animal? But where's his hooves and his horns to let the world know it's not his mother's fault? It's the man, it's the father in him spawned the devil! But who is it that pays? The mother! The poor suffering mother. [*She turns sharply to JANE.*] You've never had a husband?

JANE: No.

KATHLEEN: Then you can't know anything about a woman's life.

JANE: I'm sorry.

KATHLEEN: It's cruel, that's what it is. It's a cruel joke, this Devil Baby.

JANE: It seems to be.

KATHLEEN: Well, it's not your fault. You don't know anything about it. [*She rises.*] I'll take my knife back now. It's the only one I have for cutting bread, when I've got the bread to cut. [*JANE retrieves it from the drawer and hands it to her. KATHLEEN takes it thoughtfully.*] You know, this is the first time I ever used a knife against a living soul. I should have done it years ago. [*She turns to go.*]

JANE: You can use the door.

KATHLEEN: [*Turning*] Miss Addams—you teach a lot of girls at Hull House, don't you?

JANE: Yes.

KATHLEEN: Teach them there's no Devil Baby. Teach them not to wait for it. [*She holds up the knife to salute JANE who opens the door for her. KATHLEEN exits, and JANE stands watching her as the lights fade.*]

THE END

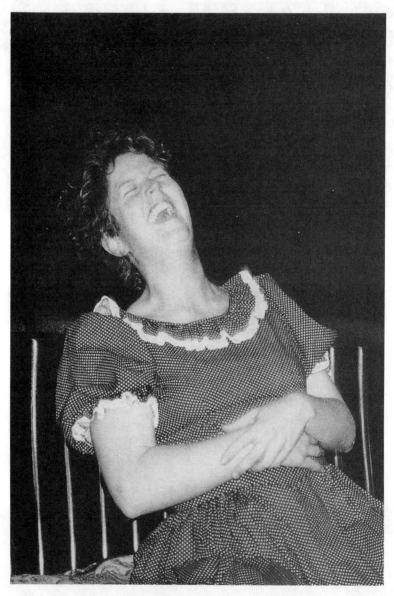

"You're not serious? Louisa!" A lesbian Jo March (Sue Carney) howls at Louisa's naive attempt to marry her off to Professor Bhaer in *Louisa May Incest*.

Louisa May Incest
A One-Act Play For Two Women

Cast of Characters

LOUISA MAY ALCOTT—A woman of thirty-five.
JO MARCH—A woman in her early twenties with short hair.

The scene is Louisa May Alcott's room in Orchard House, Concord, 1868.

LOUISA MAY INCEST

The scene is Louisa May Alcott's room in Orchard House, Concord, 1868. Her father, Bronson Alcott, has his study across the hall. LOUISA MAY is thirty-five years old. She sits at a writing table and takes out her manuscript, pens, ink, and paper. Then she closes the curtains and crosses to the door to lock it. She sits down and begins to write. Someone is heard trying the door handle. Finding it locked, the outsider tries to force the lock. Then she knocks. Finally she calls out.

JO: [*Offstage*] Louisa! Louisa! I can't get in! The door must be locked. [*LOUISA looks up from her work, disturbed, but she resolves to ignore the voice. She continues to work.*] Louisa! Can you hear me? Louisa! It's me, Jo! [*She rattles the knob.*] Louisa! I can hear you . . . What's the matter? Is someone else there? Louisa? Are you all right? Louisa, answer me! I'm going to break the door down. [*JO begins to batter the door. LOUISA, frightened, sits at her desk. She tries to ignore it.*] Don't worry, Louisa, I'm coming . . . [*Suddenly the door gives, and JO rushes in. JO is JO MARCH from* Little Women. *She is in her early twenties, with very short hair. Jo trips, landing at Louisa's feet.*] Louisa! Louisa, are you all right? [*She throws her arms around the older woman.*] What's the matter, dearest? Why was the door locked? [*LOUISA looks away.*] Oh, Louisa, you weren't thinking those glum thoughts again, were you? Why didn't you call for me earlier? Is it your family again? It was Bronson, wasn't it? I saw the light on in his study across the hall. It was your father, wasn't it? He's been criticizing you again, hasn't he?

LOUISA: No. It has nothing to do with my family.

JO: What is it, darling? You know I'd do anything in the world for you. Is it one of your publishers? I know a thing or two about those men. It is, isn't it?

LOUISA: No, it's not.

JO: [*She sees the manuscript out on the table.*] It's *Little Women*, then, isn't it? You're depressed about how it's going. Well, of course you are. You've been pegging away at it for months, day and night. Of course, you're tired. After all, you're human. Me, I could just rattle along forever, telling stories and blundering through. But of course, it's not the same for you. You need to eat and sleep. I've been so thoughtless. It's all my fault. Whenever you want to work, I just get so excited about the book, I get started, and I don't know when to stop. You see, I'm doing it now. You just turn and say, "Jo March, that's enough now," and I'll stop right where I am. Oh, I can see now that you haven't been taking enough time to rest. And you haven't had lunch, have you? . . . and it's nearly four . . .

LOUISA: It isn't me. I'm fine.

JO: Well, you dear, of course you'd say that if a ton of bricks fell on your head. That's just what I would say too, so I know. But you can't fool me, Louisa May Alcott. You can't fool your Jo. You've been working too hard.

LOUISA: No, I haven't.

JO: . . . But you think your family needs the money, so you're racing to finish the book. That's exactly what I would do—but it isn't right. You deserve a rest. We'll work on this tomorrow. Today, you just take a walk out in the sunshine, and eat a big healthy dinner . . . and I don't care what your father says, a little red meat wouldn't do you any harm . . . and you go to bed early—no reading! And tomorrow, bright and early, when you come into the study, I'll be waiting for you, and we'll start right in. You'll see. We'll work so hard tomorrow, because we'll be fresh, that we'll get twice as much done—and you won't have lost any work from today. Now, go on. Get your hat. Go on. I'll be waiting here.

LOUISA: I'm not tired. And I don't want to go out. And I don't want you to wait here. [*JO is surprised by the sharpness in her voice.*] I want to finish the book without you.

JO: [*After a long pause*] You mean I'm going to die like Beth?

LOUISA: [*Avoiding her eyes*] You're not going to die. You're the main character.

JO: Then I don't understand. I thought we were writing this together.

LOUISA: We were. But I need to finish it alone.

JO: It's my dreadful language, isn't it—all that slang? "Christopher Columbus" and . . .

LOUISA: No, it's not the slang.

JO: Yes, it is. I know. And my selfishness.

LOUISA: [*Smiling*] You're not selfish, Jo.

JO: Oh, yes, I am. I'm not at all generous like Marmee, or Beth . . . and I've never learned to cook like Meg, and I'm not the least bit artistic like Amy . . .

LOUISA: You're fine, Jo.

JO: No, I'm not a bit. And I don't blame you at all for wanting to work without me. There—that's what I deserve for being so vain about my writing. And all I've published is a few stories in the *Weekly Volcano*. And here I've been thinking I can write a real book with a real author.

Well, I don't blame you a bit, Louisa. And I'm grateful you let me work with you as long as you did, although, of course, I should have seen it couldn't last. Well, there—that's enough of that, Josephine March! Now you just stop feeling sorry for yourself and get back to your own work. [*She rises.*]

LOUISA: Jo, wait. [*JO turns.*] Come back.

JO: I don't want to keep you from your writing.

LOUISA: There's plenty of time for that. Come here. [*JO returns to her side.*] Oh, Jo, I'm going to miss you. [*She hugs her.*]

JO: [*Rallying*] Well, it's not like I'll be gone forever. I'll come back when the book is finished, and you can tell me all about it, and we'll celebrate. And maybe by then I will have published something of my own—and you can be proud of me.

LOUISA: I am proud of you.

JO: Oh, Louisa, I don't deserve it, but I do so much love it when you say things like that. [*She sits at her feet.*]

LOUISA: [*Reaching down and rumpling her hair*] Look at this hair!

JO: It's growing back.

LOUISA: I like it short.

JO: So do I. [*She catches LOUISA's hand.*] Is your hand still cramped?

LOUISA: It's not too sore today.

JO: Let me work on it. [*She massages her writing hand.*] How does that feel?

LOUISA: Better.

JO: I could still come every day and work on your hand. I could help you that way . . .

LOUISA: No.

JO: Why? I know I'm not as good a writer as you, but I could still help you in other ways. And I can be very quiet. Really.

LOUISA: Dear Jo. I won't be able to finish the book if you're here.

JO: Why not?

LOUISA: Because it's time for you to start growing up.

JO: [*Getting up quickly from the floor and sitting in a chair*] I am growing up. I just forget sometimes.

LOUISA: I'm not talking about your sitting on the floor.

JO: [*Looking down*] I know what you're talking about.

LOUISA: You do?

JO: Of course. I think about it all the time when I'm by myself. I know you're disappointed in my writing. So am I. I haven't been working on it nearly as much as I should. And mostly I've been trying to write those stories that will sell. And I know you're thinking it's time I took my work more seriously, if I'm to become a successful writer by the end of the book. Here we are three hundred pages along, and I still haven't done anything.

LOUISA: [*Looking away*] It's not your writing.

JO: Don't try to be tactful. I know. But now that I've moved away from home to the rooming house, I'll be able to work better. There won't be so many interruptions . . .

LOUISA: That's not what I meant when I said you needed to grow up.

JO: I don't understand.

LOUISA: I need to make plans for your future.

JO: I'm going to be a writer like you. [*LOUISA says nothing.*] I thought that was obvious. It's right there on the very first page about how much I love books. And then there's that little collection of children's stories I've written. And the Pickwick Club, and how I was the editor of the Club's paper. Everyone has always known that I would be a writer. I'm going to write a great book someday and make lots of money, just like you.

LOUISA: You need a family.

JO: I have a family . . . Amy, Meg . . .

LOUISA: Meg is married.

JO: She's still my family.

LOUISA: [*Smiling*] You never could accept losing her.

JO: [*Defensive*] Just because she got married, she's still my sister.

LOUISA: Jo, you need a family of your own.

JO: [*Sitting in silence for a minute*] Louisa, I thought you agreed that I wouldn't have to marry Laurie. You said that Amy was going to marry him.

LOUISA: She is.

JO: Then what are you talking about? You're two thirds the way through the book and there isn't anybody else for me to marry—unless it's Laurie's grandfather, old Mr. Laurence.

LOUISA: It's not Mr. Laurence.

JO: Well, then it's too late now. You can't introduce a new character this late in the book. Your readers would never believe it. I'm just going to stay in my rooming house until I sell my first book. And then I'm going to buy a house big enough for Marmee and Amy . . .

LOUISA: There is someone else. [*JO looks at her.*] Someone in the rooming house.

JO: [*She looks confused for a moment until she realizes what LOUISA has in mind.*] You're not serious! Louisa! [*LOUISA looks away.*] That seedy German professor? Louisa?

LOUISA: You like him.

JO: I like him, but I'm not going to marry him. He's old enough to be my father!

LOUISA: [*Alarmed, she crosses to the door and closes it.*] This is what I mean about our not being able to work together any more.

JO: Friedrich Bhaer is shabby, and repulsive, and bigoted, and doesn't take care of himself, and he can hardly speak English!

LOUISA: He's German.

JO: And he has two children, two *boys*.

LOUISA: They're his nephews.

JO: But *he's* raising them.

79

LOUISA: He loves children.

JO: I can't believe you're serious about this. It must be some kind of joke. Louisa—[*LOUISA has turned away.*] Louisa, talk to me!

LOUISA: There's no point in discussing it if you're going to be hysterical.

JO: [*Scared*] What have I done, Louisa? I've been too wild, haven't I? I've been too lazy? I'll do better. I'm going to sit myself down and write for eight hours a day. See if I don't. Just give me one year at the rooming house. If by then I haven't published a book, you can marry me off to anybody in the world, and I won't say a word. I promise. Just give me a year.

LOUISA: Jo, it isn't a punishment. He's a good man.

JO: So is Laurie, but I don't have to marry him.

LOUISA: Laurie is a boy. The Professor is a man.

JO: An old man.

LOUISA: A mature man. You need someone mature.

JO: Why?

LOUISA: Because you lack moral judgment.

JO: [*Angry*] What does that mean?

LOUISA: You don't always do the right thing. You go by your feelings too much.

JO: I don't feel like marrying that seedy, self-righteous bigot.

LOUISA: I'm not surprised. Feelings are usually selfish.

JO: [*Shouting*] That's not selfish! How would you like to marry him? [*LOUISA turns back to her papers, ignoring JO. JO struggles to get control of her feelings.*] I'm sorry. [*She sits.*]

LOUISA: [*Looking up*] I've chosen Professor Bhaer because of his maturity. He has the wisdom to help you become the woman you want to be.

JO: How is he going to do that? Teach me German? [*LOUISA turns away again.*] I'm sorry, Louisa. How is he going to help me?

LOUISA: He is going to keep you aware of what is really important in life.

JO: And what is really important in life?

LOUISA: Serving others.

JO: [*Exploding*] I do! That's all I've ever done! Louisa—this move to the rooming house is the first time I've ever even begun to have a life of my own! And this money I've begun to earn for writing stories—that's the first time I've ever had a taste of being independent!

LOUISA: I don't think the rooming house was a good idea. I'm afraid that when I wrote that chapter, I was a little carried away by your ideas.

JO: What are you talking about?

LOUISA: Those stories you write.

JO: What about them?

LOUISA: Are you proud of them?

JO: [*Defensively*] I'm proud of the money.

LOUISA: [*Looking away*] This is why you need Professor Bhaer.

JO: What's he got to do with my writing?

LOUISA: He's going to make you see what you're doing to yourself by writing those trashy stories for money.

JO: He can't do that.

LOUISA: [*Smiling*] He already has.

JO: [*Looks at her for a moment, and then looks at the manuscript on the desk*] You've written it! You've written it in without me! [*She grabs the top paper and begins to read it.*] "I would more rather give my boys gun-powder to play with than this bad trash!" That moralizing, pompous, conceited jackass! He doesn't have a family of six to support! How dare he . . .

LOUISA: [*Rising, flushed*] Give them back.

JO: [*She continues to read.*] "If respectable people knew what harm they did, they would not feel then the living was honest." How dare he say that to me? Does he have any idea what I would have to be doing if I wasn't writing these stories? Does he have the faintest idea of how hard it is for a woman to make money? Has he ever been a live-in companion? Does he think it's more honorable to live in some stranger's home, to be treated like a slave, to put up with the sexual advances of every male in the household? Is that his idea of moral, just because *I'm* the victim? Has he ever taken in sewing for a living? I don't see him exactly making money, and he's a man, and thirty years older than me, and a professor at that! Do you know what things I would be doing if I were a man? Do you know what I would do if I could have gone to college and gotten a degree? You can believe I wouldn't be living in some broken-down

82

rooming house, giving German lessons for a living! Louisa—think of it! Think what women like us would be doing if we had been allowed to go to college!

LOUISA: You're wrong about Professor Bhaer. He's a great man. Now, give those back.

JO: [*Reading again*] "Jo . . . stuffed the whole bundle into her stove . . ." [*She looks up.*] I *burn* my writing? [*LOUISA tries to snatch the papers, but JO dodges her.*] I *burn* my own writing, because of what this self-righteous lecher says?

LOUISA: [*She finally succeeds in retrieving the papers.*] This is why it's impossible for us to collaborate.

JO: I can't believe it. I *burn* my own writing?

LOUISA: Yes. [*Avoiding her eyes*] Like the way you cut off your hair.

JO: It's not the same thing.

LOUISA: Yes, it is. It's for a higher principle.

JO: No, it isn't. Hair grows back. Louisa, don't you remember how I wouldn't even speak to Amy when she got mad at me and burned that little book of stories? You had to almost drown her to make me feel like forgiving her. Remember? And now you're going to expect me to take my own writings—that pay the rent—and *burn* them? I wouldn't do it.

LOUISA: You will do it. I've written it.

JO: No, I won't. I won't do it. You can write it, but I won't be there. And all your readers will know.

LOUISA: You'll do it, because it's the right thing to do.

JO: What about you? Would you burn your own writing? Would you burn *Little Women*?

LOUISA: I don't need to. It's a children's story. It isn't trash.

JO: What about your romance stories?

LOUISA: I don't have any.

JO: Oh, Louisa, don't lie to me. I know you. Where do you think I stole my plots from?

LOUISA: I don't know what you're talking about.

JO: [*Angry*] Oh, don't you . . . "Flora Fairfield," "A. M. Barnard . . . ?" [*LOUISA freezes.*] Those are your pen names, aren't they? The ones you used when you wrote "The Rival Painters," "The Abbot's Ghost," "Pauline's Passion . . ."

LOUISA: [*Cutting her off*] Where did you find those?

JO: I didn't need to find them. They're in your head, Louisa. I know you better than you know me.

LOUISA: I have had to support a real family. Yours is make-believe. It's different.

JO: How?

LOUISA: How? All I have to do is write a sentence, and suddenly you've sold a story. It's not that easy for me. I have to write it. I have to send it out. It gets returned, it gets lost, nobody buys it. That's real life, Jo. That's my life. You should thank me that I have decided you don't have to struggle the way I have. I'm going to have your Aunt March die and leave you her estate. Nobody is going to do that for me. Nobody's going to write a happy ending for me.

JO: Maybe I don't want a happy ending. Maybe I choose to write, because I love it. Maybe I'm just like you.

LOUISA: [*Bitterly*] I write for the money.

JO: Don't lie to me, Louisa. You write those thriller stories for the same reason I do—because you like to. You get to say all kinds of unladylike things. You get to kill men. You get to pretend you're a man and write about laying your head against a woman's breast . . .

LOUISA: [*Agitated*] Jo! What are you talking about?

JO: I'm talking about you—about us! You wish you could live like a man just as much as I do.

LOUISA: No, I don't.

JO: Where do you think I get my ideas from? You call me "fellow," you cut all my hair off, you call me the man of the family. I use slang, I race Laurie and beat him, I give my money to support the family, I'm wildly jealous of John for marrying Meg. Louisa, you know what I am as well as I do. That's why I can't get married.

LOUISA: You're a tomboy. You just need to grow up.

JO: Look again, Louisa. You need to grow up. I'm a lesbian.

LOUISA: No! No, you're not!

JO: Yes, I am. Remember what you had me tell Laurie—"It's impossible for people to make themselves love other people if they don't . . ." Remember? We told him, "I don't believe it's the right sort of love, and I'd rather not try it." You know why I said that.

LOUISA: Laurie was a friend, but I never intended those remarks to refer to all men.

JO: Louisa, you know I love women. You know that. You know because you created me out of your own need to love women.

LOUISA: I don't want to love them like that.

JO: Oh yes, you do, Louisa May Alcott. And you want them to love you like that.

LOUISA: No!

JO crosses to LOUISA. She takes her hand, the writing hand, and caresses it. LOUISA closes her eyes. JO takes her hand and brings it to her lips. She begins to kiss and caress her fingers.

JO: Louisa, you are so beautiful. You take care of everybody. Who takes care of you? Nobody sees you like I do. I see who you are—I see how beautiful you are. Let me love you, Louisa. [*She kisses her lips. LOUISA, after the kiss, turns away in confusion.*]

LOUISA: I was in love with David.

JO: Louisa . . .

LOUISA: I was. I would have married him.

JO: Henry David Thoreau despised women, and you know it. He liked little boys.

LOUISA: I loved him.

JO: You loved him, because you knew you'd never have to do anything about it.

LOUISA: And I loved Ladislas.

JO: That boy you met three years ago in Switzerland?

LOUISA: I was in love with him.

JO: You were infatuated. He was eighteen. You were thirty-three. You were attracted to him, because he was the closest thing to a woman you could find.

LOUISA: [*Turning to look at JO*] No! You're twisting things.

JO: Louisa, you're the one twisting things. Look at who you pick to fall in love with—homosexual men and adolescent boys!

LOUISA: [*Rising*] No!

JO: Yes! The reason you have never married, is because you're a lesbian. Like me. [*She puts her arms around LOUISA.*]

LOUISA: No! No . . .

JO: Louisa, I love you. I'm the only one who has ever loved you. That's what you created me for.

LOUISA: I created you for Professor Bhaer.

JO: You created me for your own pleasure.

LOUISA: [*Pulling away*] No. I created you to marry him.

JO: [*Nuzzling LOUISA's neck*] I can't do that, and you don't want me to.

LOUISA: Yes, yes I do. Jo, he's kind. He needs you.

JO: You need me.

87

LOUISA: [*Desperate*] You'll inherit Plumfield. You won't have to write.

JO: I'm going to stay and work with you. [*She kisses LOUISA's lips.*]

LOUISA: [*Pulling away*] You *have* to marry him.

JO: Louisa! Think about what you're asking. Think of the wedding night!

LOUISA: I'm not going to write about that.

JO: But your readers are going to think about it. Think of his seedy trousers coming down. Think of that big pink-grey penis coming out, sticking out like an elephant's trunk . . .

LOUISA: Stop it!

JO: Think about his bad breath in my face, his hairy stomach lying over my body. Think about his grunting and sweating and rocking back and forth. That's what marriage is about!

LOUISA: It's a union of two souls! It's a lifetime of companionship!

JO: It's him lying on top of me every night and shooting his sperm between my legs!

LOUISA: [*Delirious*] I'm leaving. [She heads for the door.]

JO: Why? You can't bear to hear about it, but I'm supposed to go through with it? Is that your idea of being grown up? [*LOUISA exits and JO shouts after her.*] Just because your father violated you, don't violate me!

LOUISA: [*Returning quickly and closing the door*] That's a lie!

88

JO: Oh, Louisa, come on!

LOUISA: My father is a good and pure and true man. He's one of the most highly evolved souls in Cambridge. Ask anyone here.

JO: You hate him.

LOUISA: I aspire to be like him.

JO: You hate him.

LOUISA: No, you hate him. You're jealous.

JO: I do hate him. I hate him for what he's done to you. It's bad enough that he penetrated your vagina when you were a child, but it's penetrating your brain I can't forgive him for.

LOUISA: You don't know what you're talking about.

JO: Why do you think he lost all those schools?

LOUISA: Because his ideas on educating children were ahead of his time.

JO: He lost the school in Cheshire because he invited the children to his rooms after school, and he was caught "caressing" the girls.

LOUISA: That's a lie.

JO: No, it isn't. Remember how he lost Temple School, because he wanted to talk about sex to the children?

LOUISA: He was honest and uninhibited.

JO: Was that why he would spend hours in the bath with you? Is that why he wrote when you were four months old about your "beautiful proportions," your "perfect picture of luxuriant childhood," the "boldness and amplitude" of your body? Is that why he slept with you at night? Is that why your mother was desperate to place you in another home when you were two?

LOUISA: He was a loving father.

JO: What about that dream you keep having over and over? The nightmare with the man in the cape with the soft hands, saying, "Lie still, my dear!" The man who is always coming after you out of closets, in at windows . . . the man who threatens you all night long. Where do you think you got that nightmare?

LOUISA: Dreams don't mean anything.

JO: And how about your father's writing. Have you ever read his books? How about *Observations on the Life of My Second Child, Louisa May Alcott, During the First Year?* Have you read about his little experiments with you and your sister? How your loving father would burn Anna's hand to record her reaction? Or how he would take her to the park and then hide, to see what she would do? Do you really believe he didn't perform other kinds of experiments?

LOUISA: I don't believe it.

JO: It's a fact.

LOUISA: How do you know?

JO: Because you know.

LOUISA: No, I don't.

JO: Yes, you do. You just won't open those parts of your mind. But I can see all of you, because I don't need to protect Bronson. In fact, I would like to kill him.

90

LOUISA: Jo! Don't say that! If he died, I would.

JO: That's probably true, because he's god in your brain. I can help you. We can find a happy ending together, Louisa. I can help you expose your father and get him out of your life. Here . . . take these chapters you wrote without me. Professor Bhaer doesn't belong in our book. He's your father. Take these and burn them.

LOUISA: Now you expect me to burn my work.

JO: You didn't really write these. Bronson dictated them to you. Professor Bhaer is his alter-ego. Burn them. Burn them, Louisa, and we'll rewrite the ending where I meet a wonderful older woman who is a writer, and we collaborate on a children's book about four sisters and their mother, and it becomes a great success, and we buy a house together, and we continue to write books, and we meet all the brightest women in Boston, and they come to our house every week for salons . . . forever and ever.

LOUISA: [*Taking the chapters, she moves towards the fireplace.*] I could be one of the boarders at the rooming house.

JO: You could. We could read to each other what we've written every evening.

LOUISA: You would sleep with me?

JO: [*Cautiously*] We could.

LOUISA: No. [*She stops.*] No, I see what's going on here. You are tempting me. [*LOUISA begins to speak in a style of oratory she has picked up from her father.*] You, my creation, are the personification of all my worst weaknesses. This is my selfishness, my self-indulgence, my carnal desires speaking to me. I know you, Jo March—you are my own worst self.

91

JO: Your best self, Louisa! You are talking like Bronson now. He wants to ruin your life. He's taken thirty-five years already. He's a vampire. He sucks your life blood, and now he's sucking your creative blood. Don't let him, Louisa! Burn these chapters.

LOUISA: [*Becoming very distant and rhetorical*] Oh, you're clever, Jo March. I might have known you would be. I was always able to fool myself. If it weren't for the firm moral foundation my father laid in me, I might be tempted to listen to you. But thankfully I have his strong example to guide me. Without him, I would steer like a ship without a rudder, giving in to my impulses at every instant, headed nowhere at all and wrecking myself on the treacherous shoals of self-gratification.

JO: [*She grabs LOUISA's shoulders.*] What are you talking about? Living your own life is not a crime.

LOUISA: You're a clever temptress.

JO: Louisa, your father is a child molester.

LOUISA: You must be very weak to malign such a good man.

JO: He is! You know it! Every sentence you write reeks of incest!

LOUISA: Poor Jo—your father was away, wasn't he, and you're jealous that I have always lived so close to mine. You can't understand what it is to have a saint for a father.

JO: A saint! Bronson Alcott is a devil! [*She grabs the chapters.*]

LOUISA: [*Gently*] You know you can't act without my permission. You are my creation.

JO: I know that deep down you want me to burn these. I know that's what's in your heart. [*She crosses to the fireplace. LOUISA watches her. JO picks up the matches and freezes.*] Louisa, please. I know you must want to be happy.

LOUISA: My father has taught me the way to happiness is self-sacrifice.

JO: [*Frantic*] That's the way to *his* happiness. When have you ever seen Bronson do anything for anybody else? Haven't you and your mother been supporting him for twenty years? What has he ever done for his family except molest and abandon you?

LOUISA: [*Not hearing her*] You see, you can't burn them. I don't want you to. You will put them on my desk. [*JO obeys.*]

JO: This means I will have to burn my work. It's in this chapter.

LOUISA: Yes, you will. It's the right thing.

JO: Oh, Louisa, you have killed us both.

LOUISA: *Little Women* will be a great success.

JO: Only in a world of incest.

LOUISA: I think you can go now.

JO: I'll never come back.

LOUISA: That's as it should be. The Professor will need you more than I do.

JO: You and your book are poisoned.

LOUISA: [*Smiling*] Oh, I forgot to tell you . . . You and the Professor are going to turn Plumfield into a school for little boys.

JO turns to look at her a final time. Silently she exits, closing the door behind her. LOUISA crosses after her, locks the door, and returns to the manuscript. Lights fade.

THE END

Battered on Broadway
A Vendetta in One Act

Cast of Characters

NELLIE FORBUSH DEBECQUE, from *South Pacific*
BESS, from *Porgy and Bess*
MEI LI, from *Flower Drum Song*
ALDONZA, from *Man of La Mancha*
MARIA, from *West Side Story*
JULIE, from *Carousel*
SALLY BOWLES, from *Cabaret*
ORPHAN ANNIE, from *Annie*
MAID
NUN

The setting is Mame's Manhattan penthouse. The time is late morning, the present.

"I've got more freedom bein' dead!" Sally Bowles from *Cabaret* (Akia Woods) enjoys a private laugh with the friend she has introduced as Guinevere from *Camelot* (Natalie Garrett) in *Battered on Broadway*.

BATTERED ON BROADWAY

The scene takes place in the living room of Mame's lavish Manhattan penthouse.

NELLIE FORBUSH DEBECQUE is hosting a reunion for women from former Broadway hit musicals. Most of the women are in their fifties or sixties, depending on their age in the musical and the year the musical opened.

The women are: BESS from Porgy and Bess, *MEI LI from* Flower Drum Song, *ALDONZA from* Man of La Mancha, *MARIA from* West Side Story, *JULIE from* Carousel, *and SALLY BOWLES from* Cabaret. *There is a NUN present, presumably Guinevere from* Camelot.

The women are standing around in groups, laughing and talking. The MAID enters with a coffee service and begins to pour. NELLIE checks her watch, and dismisses the MAID.

NELLIE: [*Clinking her spoon against her cup*] Ladies! Ladies. . . . May I have your attention, please? [*They give her their attention.*] Thank you. I think we're ready to begin here. First I'd like us to introduce ourselves, and then Julie here is going to talk about the project that we're here to organize. Let me say, it's wonderful to be back here in New York, and it's so wonderful to see all of you again—after so many years. I think it's been twenty years since I saw you, Bess.

BESS: Thirty, honey. But when the reporters get here, we'll tell them twenty.

SALLY BOWLES: When is the press going to arrive?

NELLIE: In about a half hour. I thought we could all get through our business first, and then they could join us for the luncheon buffet and take candid shots during that. I know how we all hate this kind of invasion, but I think it's really important for the success of our fund-raising that we have this kind of publicity. But anyone who doesn't want to be interviewed or photographed can leave before they get here.

ALDONZA: Who is coming?

NELLIE: *Time, Life, Newsweek, The Washington Post, The New York Times,* and all three major networks . . . and "All Things Considered."

BESS: Didn't leave anyone out, did you?

NELLIE: Not if I could help it.

JULIE: Are they all going to fit in here?

SALLY BOWLES: In Mame's penthouse? Are you kidding? She used to invite half of Manhattan to her parties.

BESS: That's the truth. Where is that girl anyway?

NELLIE: She's off exploring the Himalayas with Vera, but she's very supportive of the project. That's why she loaned us her penthouse for the reunion.

BESS: The Himalayas! Mame must be in her eighties!

SALLY BOWLES: She wanted to do them before she got too old.

NELLIE: Well, let's start with introductions. I'm Nellie Forbush DeBecque, from *South Pacific.* [*She turns to JULIE.*]

JULIE: And I'm Julie Jordan from *Carousel*.

BESS: Bess from *The Sound of Music*. [*They all laugh appreciatively.*] No, wait—*Porgy and Bess*. With all the Black musicals they have on Broadway, I keep getting it confused.

MARIA: Maria from *West Side Story*.

SALLY BOWLES: [*Giving herself a Joel Grey introduction*] Fraulein Sally Bowles! From *Cabaret*. And this is my friend Guinevere from *Camelot*. Guinny has taken vows of silence, you know. [*The NUN bows in acknowledgment*.]

ALDONZA: I am Aldonza, la prostituta from "El hombre de la Mancha."

MEI LI: Mrs. Wang Ta, formerly Mei Li from *Flower Drum Song*.

NELLIE: It's just wonderful to see all of you here today. And I know some of you have had to travel quite a distance to be here—Guinevere and Sally have flown in from London, and Aldonza from Spain. Mrs. Ta lives in San Francisco . . . I know what an effort you have all made to be here, and I'm grateful for your commitment to the project. And now I'm going to let Julie tell you about that, because it was her idea.

JULIE: [*Rising, she speaks to NELLIE.*] Thank you, Nellie. If it weren't for your help in organizing the reunion, I couldn't have done it. I'll never know how you managed to track down everybody after so many years. [*To the others*] But there's one woman we couldn't invite today, and that woman represents why we're here. I'm sure we all remember Nancy Sikes. [*There is a murmur of assent.*] Nancy is not here today, because Nancy is dead. She was beaten to death by her husband, on-stage, in the musical *Oliver!* Those of us who saw it opening night will never forget it. [*Pause*] Nancy's death should not have been a surprise. It had been coming for a long time. Not many people will remember, but I was also a battered wife. It didn't happen on-stage, like with Nancy, but I talked about it. In the second act my daughter came to me because her father had hit her, and I told her that when some men hit you, it feels like a kiss. [*The women respond with shock.*] And for those of us who were not actually battered in our shows, we were surrounded by it. I think of Anna in *The King and I.* Every other woman in that play was in sexual or domestic slavery to the king of Siam. And how was she supposed to react? She taught him ballroom dancing! How many of us were expected to give up our dreams and ideals to meet the selfish desires of worthless men—men who represented the opposite of everything we stood for. What happened to Marion in *The Music Man?* All she wanted was a quiet, gentle partner who could talk to her about Shakespeare. What did she get? A traveling salesman who made his living by selling nonexistent band instruments to children! And Sarah from *Guys and Dolls*, a woman committed to fighting a war on alcoholism and gambling addictions . . . Who did she have to marry? Skye Masterson—a professional gambler and an alcoholic. And Liza Doolittle—spunky little Liza . . . She closed her own show by fetching slippers for her master like some kind of dog. Nellie?

NELLIE: My story is a familiar one, too. My first taste of freedom was also my last. I was away from home for the first time, supporting myself, living in a wonderful community of army nurses—having the time of my life—and what happens? I'm supposed to want to give it all up to go live on a plantation with a man twice my age, and raise his children for him!

ALDONZA: [*Facetiously*] Pobrecita! [*MARIA laughs. NELLIE is surprised and offended.*]

JULIE: [*Making peace*] All of us here know what it is to be victimized by a script that is written from the point of view of rich white men. We know what it is to say lines that betray ourselves, to give up our lives to serve inferior men, to participate in our own abuse. We know that we did these things not because we were stupid, not because we were masochistic, not because we wanted to. We did them because we had to. We did them because we had no one to turn to, nowhere else to go.

Nancy Sikes died, because she had no support in her efforts to save Oliver. If there had been some shelter where she could have gone, Nancy would be with us today. This is why I would like to see us, victims of Broadway's earlier misogyny, raise the money for a Broadway Battered Women's Shelter. [*The women applaud. Suddenly the bell rings.*]

NELLIE: I'll get it, Julie. You go on. [*The MAID enters, but NELLIE waves her away. She lingers at the tea table, eavesdropping.*]

JULIE: I feel this is an opportunity for me to correct the damage done by my role in *Carousel.* I feel that this is a chance for me to do something for the younger women who are coming along now . . . [*NELLIE has received a telegram and is reading it.*]

NELLIE: Wait, Julie! Listen! [*She reads.*] "I regret that my daughter will be unable to attend your luncheon . . ." [*SALLY makes eye contact with the MAID.*] ". . . Am wiring ten million dollars to your account. Hope this will be of some service to the Battered Women's Project. Best of luck." [*SALLY crosses to the MAID, whispers to her, and the MAID exits.*]

JULIE: Ten million dollars . . .

SALLY BOWLES: Who's it from?

NELLIE: Daddy Warbucks.

BESS: That man has got money.

JULIE: He's the richest man in the world.

SALLY BOWLES: I wonder why Annie didn't respond herself.

NELLIE: I don't know, but this is certainly a windfall.

MARIA: Does this mean you don't have to raise any more money?

101

NELLIE: This will cover the cost of buying the site and building the shelter. We would still have to raise the funds for operating expenses. I'm sorry, Julie. I'm afraid I interrupted you.

JULIE: No, I was just finishing up anyway. I would like to get some feedback from the rest of you about the project.

BESS: Sounds like a good idea to me. I came up here with that pimp Sportin' Life, and an armful of drugs. Took me ten years to get clean and get free of that bastard.

ALDONZA: You were a prostitute?

BESS: A working girl, honey.

ALDONZA: Don't be ashamed of it. I was a prostitute. Today in Spain I organize the girls who work in the sex trades. We are not ashamed. We work for our money, and when we have it, it's our own. Where's the shame?

MEI LI: I was a mail order bride.

ALDONZA: You see? You show me the women who don't have to suck dick to live, and then I will be ashamed to be a prostitute.

MARIA: Lesbians.

ALDONZA: What about lesbians?

MARIA: The women who don't have to sell themselves to men.

ALDONZA: Don't tell me that! Half of the prostitutas are lesbians.

MARIA: My lover and I, we don't work for men. We don't live with them, we don't go out with them, we don't talk to them. We don't have anything to do with them.

ALDONZA: So where does your money come from?

MARIA: We have a karate school for women, and we publish a magazine for Latina lesbians.

ALDONZA: And with this you make big money.

MARIA: Not big money. But we can live.

ALDONZA: To live! Women want more than just to live! We want our cars. We want our houses. We want some good clothes for the children. We want to eat well. Maybe even go to a restaurant every now and then. Buy a few flowers. To live! To live with nothing is sucking on the dick!

MARIA: No, it's not!

ALDONZA: Don't tell me! They gonna stick it to you one way or another. Don't tell Aldonza about fairy tales. Tell them to Dulcinea. Don't tell them to Aldonza!

BESS: We have to start somewhere. And the reason we're here is the battered women's shelter, right Nellie?

NELLIE: That's right. I was thinking . . .

ALDONZA: [Interrupting, to MARIA] Maria! Maria! What happened to your cousin?

MARIA: My cousin?

ALDONZA: The one they tried to gang rape on the stage. It was inside a store . . . with the white boys . . . you know, the Jets?

MARIA: You mean Anita.

ALDONZA: Sí, Anita. How is she?

MARIA: She's dead.

ALDONZA: Did she kill herself?

MARIA: No. It was an overdose of heroin.

ALDONZA: She killed herself.

BESS: [*Putting her hand on MARIA's arm*] That's hard. [*There is a long silence.*]

ALDONZA: [*Singing*] "Little bird, little bird / In the cinnamon tree / Little bird, little bird / Do you sing for me?" [*No one says anything. They recognize the song.*] That's the song they sang when they gang-raped me on-stage. Big party. Big men. I spit on them. I spit on the Jets. [*She spits. The doorbell rings.*]

NELLIE: Excuse me a minute. [*The MAID enters again, but NELLIE arrives at the door first and opens it. ANNIE stands there, a woman in her thirties with wild red hair and sunglasses.*]

ANNIE: Is this the Broadway reunion?

NELLIE: Yes . . . and you must be . . . ?

ANNIE: [*Taking off her hat and her sunglasses and tossing them to the MAID, who takes them, looks at SALLY, and exits.*] Annie. As in "Little." As in "Orphan." [*She sweeps into the room.*]

NELLIE: We understood you weren't coming.

ANNIE: Who told you that?

NELLIE: We got a telegram from your father.

ANNIE: My father? Warbucks is not my father. Let's get that real straight right now. He bought me. Like he buys everything. He was my owner, not my father.

NELLIE: Well, he sent a telegram saying you weren't coming.

ANNIE: Yeah, he wished. He had me all locked up snug in a private institution—paid them to keep me there. But two can play that little game. I paid them to let me out.

SALLY BOWLES: Why did he lock you up?

ANNIE: Why? Because I'm crazy—can't you tell? And I'm not cute anymore, or hadn't you noticed? Little Orphan Annie has grown up. She doesn't wear spanky pants anymore. And she talks.

SALLY BOWLES: So Warbucks had you locked up for no reason?

ANNIE: Oh, he had reasons. He had plenty of reasons. And today I'm going to tell the whole world all about them.

NELLIE: What do you mean?

ANNIE: The press is going to be here, aren't they?

JULIE: Yes.

ANNIE: Good. Good! How do I look? I don't want to look crazy, you know. I thought this little outfit would have just enough softness to make me look vulnerable, but not enough to make me look frivolous. What do you think? You know how it is with first impressions.

NELLIE: I'm sorry, Annie, but I'm not understanding what it is exactly that you're planning to do here.

ANNIE: I am planning to tell the reporters the truth about Daddy Warbucks, Daddy Bigbucks, Daddy Bumfucks. I'm going to tell them just why a rich white man who's in the business of making war, takes such an interest in rescuing little orphan girls. I'm going to tell them just what it is he does with his little sugar and spice investments.

ALDONZA: So Mr. Warbucks fucks little girls?

ANNIE: [*Looking at her*] I couldn't have said it better.

SALLY BOWLES: [*She reaches out to touch ANNIE. ANNIE whirls around with her fists up.*] I'm sorry, love. That must have been awful!

ANNIE: Don't feel sorry for me. I'm going to get my revenge. After today, the whole world is going to know the kind of man Warbucks is.

SALLY BOWLES: That could be very dangerous.

ANNIE: What could he do to me now? I've grown up. I'm a free woman. I have my own money. What could he do?

SALLY BOWLES: He could have you sued for libel. He could threaten your friends. He could have you locked up again. Actually, there's a lot of things he could do.

ANNIE: He wouldn't dare. The whole world will be watching.

NELLIE: Annie, I'm concerned that you want to use this benefit for your press conference. We're here to talk about building a battered women's shelter on Broadway.

ANNIE: And I'm here to talk about why we need one.

JULIE: But your story is so sensational, it's going to overshadow the news about the project.

NELLIE: That's what I'm thinking. I'm thinking it would be better for you to hold your own press conference.

ANNIE: No, you don't understand. I can't plan one without Daddy finding out and canceling it. No, this is perfect.

NELLIE: Well, I'm afraid I don't agree with you. This is not the right place for you to tell your story. We want the focus to be on the shelter . . . It's a separate story from your experiences with your father.

ANNIE: He's not my father. [*Looking around*] What? Do you hear this? I can't believe it! What the fuck is your shelter about if it isn't about my story? Where could an orphan girl go? And now you're telling me it's not related!

JULIE: I think what Nellie means is that we're here to save women, not to accuse men.

ANNIE: Say what? And just how do you expect to do that? If you've got a battered woman—*somebody* did the battering. How are you going to save women if you don't accuse men?

NELLIE: There are law courts for that. We are just interested in raising the money for a shelter—giving the women a place to go.

ANNIE: For what? So they can rest up for Round Two? So they can stop short of mental breakdown or death and go back to the abuser? The men are going to love that. You know what you're talking about? A recycling center for abused women. How nice. How convenient. I bet you could even get Daddy Warbucks to donate a chunk. [*An embarrassed silence*]

JULIE: Actually, he already did.

ANNIE: [*Outraged*] What?

JULIE: He already donated.

ANNIE: How much?

MARIA: Ten million.

ANNIE: [*To NELLIE*] You're not going to take it?

NELLIE: I . . . We didn't know . . . We'll have to discuss it.

ANNIE: [*To the others*] You're not going to take it! You're not going to build your shelter with Daddy Warbucks' money!

JULIE: Ten million dollars will buy and build the center, Annie. Real estate in Manhattan is very expensive. It would take us years to raise that kind of money.

ANNIE: Well, it's going to be pretty interesting explaining that to the press after I tell them about his child molesting.

NELLIE: Annie, I don't think that's a good idea.

ANNIE: And I don't think taking his money is a good idea.

NELLIE: These are two separate issues.

ANNIE: What about the rest of you? Do you think these are separate issues?

MARIA: I think we all feel your pain, Annie.

MEI LI: You have suffered a terrible wrong.

BESS: No one's arguing about that.

ALDONZA: That's why we take his fucking money. As long as the women have to suck dick, we will make the men pay for it! We will make them pay a lot of money!

ANNIE: No! You don't understand. Ten million dollars is nothing to Warbucks. It's chicken feed.

NELLIE: But it's not chicken feed to us, Annie.

ANNIE: Exactly. And that's what men like Warbucks count on. They can always buy us off.

JULIE: We're not saying you should protect him. I think you should tell the press your story . . .

MARIA: File a lawsuit!

JULIE: . . . It's just that you shouldn't tell it here today.

ANNIE: You're wrong. If I don't tell it here today, I may not have another chance.

NELLIE: I understand your feelings, but I hope you will respect ours.

ANNIE: No. Because you're wrong.

NELLIE: [*After a silence*] Then I will have to ask you to leave.

ANNIE: No.

NELLIE: Then I will have to call the security guard in the lobby and have you removed.

ANNIE: Go ahead.

JULIE: Annie, we're on the same side.

ANNIE: No, we're not. I'm on my side. You're on Warbucks' side.

JULIE: How can you say that?

NELLIE: Don't argue with her. I'm going to buzz security. [*She rises.*]

SALLY BOWLES: Wait! [*NELLIE turns.*] Let me talk to Annie for a minute—in private.

ANNIE: Nothing is going to change my mind.

SALLY BOWLES: I know that, love. I just want a minute alone with you—that's all. I know you're going to do what you're going to do.

NELLIE: I'll wait in the dining room.

SALLY BOWLES: [*To others*] Can you all wait with Nellie for a bit? Won't be long, I promise. [*They murmur assent and exit.*]

MARIA: [*Lingering*] Guinevere, are you coming?

SALLY BOWLES: [*To the NUN*] I'd like it if you stayed, actually. [*The NUN nods.*]

ANNIE: What? Is she going to pray for me? Or maybe for Warbucks?

SALLY BOWLES: [*To MARIA*] I'll join you in a minute.

MARIA: Annie, I want you to know you can call me if you need to talk to someone. [*ANNIE turns her back to MARIA. MARIA starts to leave. She turns back with a final appeal to ANNIE.*] You can call me anytime. [*She exits.*]

ANNIE: [*After a moment*] So. You're going to lecture me about being realistic.

SALLY BOWLES: Annie, do you know who this is? [*She indicates the NUN.*]

ANNIE: It's Guinevere from *Camelot*, isn't it? [*The NUN removes her glasses and her veil.*]

SALLY BOWLES: Do you recognize her?

ANNIE: No. *Camelot* was before my time.

SALLY BOWLES: This isn't Guinevere. It's Nancy Sikes—from *Oliver!*

ANNIE: I thought Nancy was dead.

NUN: [*Looking at SALLY, the NUN breaks into a powerful and raucous laugh, relaxing into a vulgar pose. When she collects herself enough to speak, it is with a Cockney accent.*] That's what they all think. [*She laughs again.*] I've been waitin' a long time to meet you, haven't I, Sally?

ANNIE: Why don't you tell them you're still alive?

NUN: Because I've got more freedom bein' dead. [*Explosive laughter. The NUN punches SALLY, who is enjoying the joke.*]

SALLY BOWLES: Do you know why she came here today?

ANNIE: No.

SALLY BOWLES: Because of you, love. All because of you. Nancy wanted to talk to you.

ANNIE: I don't understand.

NUN: We've had our eye on Warbucks and his gang for a long time.

ANNIE: You have?

111

NUN: He's behind the dirty little games in Nicaragua and Chile. He's the dodgey bastard who's been sellin' arms to South Africa. It was his little tinker toys that made the accidents at Chernobyl and Bhopal. No, I can tell you, Warbucks has been a very busy little boy.

SALLY BOWLES: Due for a spanking, he is. [*She and the NUN laugh.*]

ANNIE: [*Interrupting their joke*] Well, today the world is going to hear the truth about him.

NUN: The world is not going to hear the truth about him.

ANNIE: Yes, it is. And no one can stop me. If they throw me out of this building, I'll wait on the street for the reporters. I *am* going to tell my story. No one can stop me.

NUN: No one can stop you, dearie. No one can stop you at all. But just because you tell it, doesn't mean anyone's going to hear it.

ANNIE: Why won't they hear it?

NUN: Because they can't afford to hear it. Like you said yourself, Warbucks owns everything. People who have his money are scared of losing it, and people who don't, are scared they won't get it. They won't hear you until they have a good reason to hear you.

ANNIE: So you don't think I should do anything?

SALLY BOWLES: Let Nancy talk. [*She touches ANNIE's arm again, and again ANNIE spins around, prepared to fight. Suddenly the MAID enters with a pot of tea and a cup. She makes a long, deliberate cross to the NUN, pours her a cup, crosses in front of ANNIE, and stands by the tea table.*]

NUN: [*Smiling at the MAID*] Bill Sikes, me lovin' husband, beat me to a bloody raw pulp in *Oliver!,* and he left me for dead. If it hadn't been for my girlfriend who came lookin' for me, I would have died. It was she who took care of me all those months while I was decidin' whether or not it was worth it to live. Do you know I had to learn to walk all over again. I had to learn to talk. Couldn't remember a single bloody word for anything. Do you know who it was taught me English again? [*ANNIE doesn't answer. The NUN points to the MAID.*] May I present Liza Doolittle?

ANNIE: Liza Doolittle! From *My Fair Lady*?

MAID: [*Bowing, she speaks with a Cockney accent also.*] At your service.

NUN: Liza is a mistress of many disguises—and many voices. After I was on my feet again, the first job we pulled was Higgins' house. Cleaned the blighter out, we did. Took all his language books and records . . .

MAID: Took his bloody slippers, too.

ANNIE: He didn't know?

MAID: Oh, he knew all right. He was just too proud to report that his little human experiment had backfired on him. You know his male ego.

NUN: And then we set up shop, so to speak. Whenever we'd hear about women who'd been raped or robbed or beaten up, we'd go trackin' down the bloody bastards.

ANNIE: Would you kill them?

NUN: Let's just say they disappeared.

ANNIE: You kill men?

MAID: We save women.

ANNIE: Yes, but . . . you could go to jail!

NUN: How? Liza here's always in perfect disguise, and I'm already dead! [*She explodes in laughter.*]

ANNIE: What about Sally?

SALLY BOWLES: I've got the money, love. [*The three conspirators share a laugh.*]

ANNIE: But . . . you were in Berlin . . .

SALLY BOWLES: I left Berlin during the war, and I came back to London. I couldn't go back home to Mummy, you know—the tears and all of that muck—and I felt so guilty about the things I'd seen while I was sleeping around with those Nazi officers—well, I was feeling quite blue, actually. So one night, when I was walking by the Thames, I just took a notion to end it all, as they say. I was just taking my shoes off to jump, when this woman reaches out and grabs my arm, like this. [*She laughs.*] It was Nancy.

NUN: We'd been watchin' her, of course, since she came back. We knew she'd be very helpful to us.

SALLY BOWLES: You see, I knew a lot of Nazi secrets.

MAID: She knew where Hitler was hiding.

ANNIE: You mean you killed Hitler?

SALLY BOWLES: He killed himself, actually.

NUN: With a little persuasion.

MAID: They all kill themselves, don't they? That's how we see it. By the time they've made our list, they've become so selfish and destructive, we don't consider them human anymore.

114

SALLY BOWLES: Anyway, to make a long story short, this whole business with the Nazis was terribly exciting, and I stopped being depressed, and I realized that I didn't want to kill myself at all, but I really just wanted to kill men. I've been working with Liza and Nancy ever since.

ANNIE: So what do you want with me?

NUN: We want to help you.

ANNIE: You mean expose Warbucks?

SALLY BOWLES: *Dispose* Warbucks.

ANNIE: You want to kill him?

NUN: Don't you?

ANNIE: No . . . I mean . . . I don't think. . . . No. That's too much.

MAID: [*Crossing in close to ANNIE*] How many lives has he ruined?

ANNIE: I don't know. Hundreds, I guess.

NUN: And how many more is he going to ruin?

ANNIE: [*She pauses.*] A lot.

SALLY BOWLES: [*Crossing in to ANNIE from the other side*] Then we really can't allow him to live, can we, love?

ANNIE: [*Jumping away from SALLY and the MAID*] You're crazy. [*The NUN looks at SALLY. SALLY reaches out to touch ANNIE's arm. This time, ANNIE lets herself be touched.*] No, I'm sorry I said that.

SALLY BOWLES: [*Putting her arm around ANNIE*] It's all right, love. It's a crazy world.

NUN: Good women get killed because they're too good to fight back. Good women pray, good women sign petitions, good women march for peace. Meanwhile their sisters are gettin' raped, their planet's bein' sold out from under them for scrap, and their children are gettin' blown to bloody bits. You see, we've stopped bein' good women.

MAID: But we're effective, Annie. Very effective.

SALLY BOWLES: We'll need a lot more information on Warbucks and his friends before we can act. We have plenty on him, but we need more about his operation.

NUN: We need you to go home again. To pretend to get along with him. We'd like you to hire a new secretary for your Daddy.

MAID: Someone with a strong background in languages.

NUN: It's going to take a bit of time, but we always guarantee satisfaction.

SALLY BOWLES: Work with us, Annie. We need you.

ANNIE: [*After a pause*] Yes . . . Yes.

SALLY BOWLES: [*Embracing her*] That's a girl. You won't regret it. Besides, it's rather fun.

NUN: The world will thank you.

MAID: I'd better practice my typing.

SALLY BOWLES: Well, now that's all settled, I'll tell Nellie we're through in here. [*The MAID hands the NUN her sunglasses and head covering. The NUN puts her disguise back on.*] Nellie!

NELLIE: [*Appearing*] Yes?

SALLY BOWLES: Annie here has changed her mind. She's decided to leave before the reporters get here.

NELLIE: Oh, Annie, I'm so glad you understand our position. This is really for the best.

ANNIE: Yes, I can see that now.

SALLY BOWLES: Good girl.

ANNIE: [*To NELLIE*] Good luck building your shelter, any way you can. [*To the NUN*] And bless you, sister. [*The NUN crosses herself.*]

NELLIE: Thank you, Annie. Good luck to you too. I hope you can get some good therapy.

ANNIE: [*Smiling*] The best. [*She exits.*]

NELLIE: Well, Sally, I don't know how you did it. I was afraid we were going to have to have a very unpleasant scene on our hands.

SALLY BOWLES: Oh, don't thank me. It was our Guinny here did the miracle.

NELLIE: But how?

SALLY BOWLES: [*Shrugging*] The meek shall inherit the earth, don't you know?

THE END

Calamity Jane Sends a Message to her Daughter

A One-Act Play for One Woman

CALAMITY JANE SENDS A MESSAGE TO HER DAUGHTER

There is a simple wooden chair on the stage and next to it, a spittoon. JANE enters from the side. She is in her late forties. In spite of her debauched appearance and poor physical condition, she exudes an irrepressible vitality of spirit.

She crosses to the chair and dumps her body into it. She hitches up her pants and spreads her legs, getting comfortable. A deep guttural vibration, which seems to originate in her gut, moves up her chest and into her throat, culminating in a wad of phlegm, which Jane, with expert markswomanship, aims into the spittoon. For the first time, she looks directly at the audience.

Kinda makes ya sick, don't it? [*A thought hits her.*] You didn't expect me to swaller it, did you? [*Apparently we did. Jane grabs the spittoon and tips it in our direction.*] Look! [*She holds it up and rotates it so that the contents will be visible to every person in the room.*] Now you tell me how it's more ladylike to swaller a thing like that than to spit it out. [*Satisfied that she's made her point, she puts the spittoon back, with a snort of disgust.*] Ladies.

Jane sits back in her chair and regards her audience slowly and comprehensively, looking us right in the eye. When she is finished with her inventory, she sums up the sorry results:

Well, you're certainly not men. [*Resigning herself to the fact*] I come here tonight 'cause I want to give y'all a message to take to mah Janey for me. I can tell you know her. She looks like one of y'all. [*She reaches up under her seat and rearranges her undergarments.*] My union suit's gettin' fresh with me. [*Back to business*] Janey's mah daughter. I ain't seen her since she was a little girl. I give her up. [*She pauses, judging our reaction to this information.*] Yep. Give her up like liquor an' tabaccy. [*She snorts, enjoying her little joke.*] Naw, that ain't so. I still chew. [*She really knocks herself out with this one, and her paroxysm develops into a coughing fit, ending with another wad of phlegm landing in the spittoon. She considers our reaction.*]

Janey's a lady. Swallers her spit. Yep, they raised her real good. I give her to folks who had a lot of money. Anyway, I got a couple of things I want you to tell her for me. Things she oughtta know about her mother. [*Jane takes a flask out of her boot and unscrews the top. She takes a slug of whiskey.*]

I drink for my eyes. Helps me close 'em. [*She laughs, and then sobers up to return to her subject.*] First off, she don't know I'm her mother. You might want to set her down for that one. Kinda like findin' out you're pregnant, only backwards. So go easy on her. Get her broke to the saddle first. Maybe tell her that her mama ain't dead like they told her. An' then tell her that her mother lives out in Wyoming. An' then say how much her mama loves animals. An' then you can just natcherly ease into the part about muleskinnin' an' bullwhackin'. [*She considers for a minute.*] An' then show her mah pitchur. [*She laughs and takes a slug of whiskey.*] Sure hope she drinks.

[*Serious again*] Her real name is Jane Canarray Hickok. That's "Hickok," as in "Wild Bill." We was married, and don't you let anyone tell you different. We was married. He was my man. Me an' Bill, just like that. [*She holds two fingers together.*] An' Janey's his daughter. You tell her. [*She takes another slug of whiskey.*]

Bill was a man. A real man. Not one of your lily-livered, pasty-faced, limp-dick farmer types. Nope. Bill was every inch a man. Inch, hell . . . every *foot* a man! [*She laughs at her joke.*]

I met Bill when I was still wet behind the ears. Just a kid. See I was orphaned when I was fourteen, and I learned to hustle pretty good.

Had to. First time we met, we was in a poker game together, an' I beat him. [*She smiles.*] I beat him real bad. [*She savors the memory.*] Bill don't like to lose, 'specially with folks watchin', so he rears up an' calls me a cheater. So I says, "Hickok, you play cards so dumb I'd have to cheat to lose." An' everybody's laughin' at that one, so he pulls out his gun, an' then Molly behind the bar yells out, "Put that back, Bill! That there's a gal!"

Well, that done it. He just stands there lookin' at me like a hog starin' at a wristwatch. An' then all of a sudden he throws his gun on the table an' hollers, "Drinks for the house! I want all of y'all to drink to this here gal—the finest poker player in the Territories!"

Bill took a shine to me, an' we started keepin' each other company. Come spring we headed south down towards Abilene, an' we started workin' the border. I was his partner. Called myself "Jack of Diamonds." Between the two of us, we hustled a wagonload of money. Lost a wagonload too. An' all that time nobody knowed I was a woman . . . 'cept Bill. He knowed it all right. [*She pauses.*] I got pregnant, but I didn't want Bill to know. So I told him I was restless, an' I took off by myself up the trail to Yellowstone Valley, up to a place called Benson's Landin'. Benson's Landin' ain't there no more. They got a town called Livingston instead. [*She takes a thoughtful drink.*]

I had that baby in the dead of winter, all by myself, and I swole up like a pig after it, and I was runnin' a fever so high, I throwed the blankets off, with the water froze in the bucket right next to me! An' if misery ain't hell, I run outta liquor. I says to ole Janey, "It's every man for himself." Didn't figger either one of us was gonna make it.

I reckon it was about two days after I had that baby that Cap'n O'Neil knocks on the door of the cabin. He come lookin' to find the grave of his brother, killed somewhere around there by the injuns. The Sioux. They bothered everybody around there 'cept me. They thought I was crazy. Don't know what I ever done to give 'em that idea.

Well, anyway, I told this cap'n that I didn't know nothing 'bout his brother's grave, but if he cared to come back in a week, he could take a look at mine. I guess he figgered that was about the size of things, 'cause he went and got us some wood, and cooked me some food, and he bought me some whiskey, too. An' if good whiskey can't save ya, then you're already dead.

This O'Neil fella, he took to Janey. Started talkin' 'bout how him an' his wife couldn't have no kids, and how he would take Janey to England, get her some proper schoolin', playin' a piano and speakin' languages and all that stuff.

Mostly, though, I was thinkin' 'bout what would happen to Janey if I died, seein's how I almost just did. Nobody was gonna want her. Some family'd take her to keep like some kind of slave or somethin' and then when she was twelve or fourteen, she'd probably head out on her own like I done, an' that ain't no life for anybody. So when she was a year old, the cap'n come back, and I give her to him.

You tell Janey I was nineteen, an' I thought I was doin' the right thing. You tell her, and you tell anybody else who asks you that I still say I done the right thing.

But that ain't the point. I was talkin' about Wild Bill. I didn't see him again 'til two years later. By then I was livin' in Deadwood. '76. It was the summer of '76. I remember I was havin' a beer in Russell's saloon. I was the only woman in Deadwood they let in that saloon. Anyway, I had just stepped outside to talk to a buddy of mine, and I look up Main Street, and I think I'm dreamin' or somethin'.

Here comes Bill, ridin' his horse, him and Colorado Charlie and Bloody Dan Seymour. They come ridin' down Main Street. And they was all wearin' bran' new white Stetsons, fringed buckskins, and shiney boots. And they had so much silver on their saddles it was hard on your eyes to look at 'em. We went to every saloon in town that afternoon, an' the sight of Bill was so pretty next to me, I shot out all the mirrors.

That's what I think of when I think of Bill. . . . That summer, an' him ridin' down Main Street into Deadwood. End of that summer, he got killed. Sonofabitch McCall. Shot him from behind. [*She takes a slug of whiskey.*]

Bill. He was a man. Not like that McCall. Bill *always* shot 'em from the front. [*She softens.*] Had them long, stallion-tail mustaches down the sides of his face. Bill was my man. We was just like that, me an' Bill. [*She holds her two fingers together.*] Just like that. Don't care what people tell you. I *know.*

Them preacher's daughter types was always throwin' themselves at Bill, but they couldn't understand him. Hell, what'd they know about his life? Me, I drove a stagecoach, I fought the injuns, I rode with the cavalry . . . 'til they caught me takin' a bath. Let that be a lesson to you. I laid rail. I done everything a man's done, and maybe more. I knowed what Bill was thinkin' before he said it. I understood him. Wasn't anybody understood him better than me.

I want Janey to know that when people try to tell her he already had a wife, that's pure hog slop. Bill's wife was me. Back east he went through some tin-whistle ceremony with this lady who owned a circus, but he only done it to get himself a job, that's all. Business. That's all it was. Had a good head for business. But I was his woman. And Janey's his daughter.

The reason I ain't never told nobody is that things kinda creep up on ya when ya get older. Back then, we was just roughnecks on a toot. But times has changed now. Bill Hickok's in all the books. I want Janey to know she come from somebody famous. Her mama may have been a no-count drunk nobody, but her daddy was somebody. He was somebody all right. I'm gonna be buried next to Bill.

[*She takes another slug of whiskey.*] A man don't always go for looks, ya know. He got his outside, and his inside. A man don't always know he got an inside. But I know. I seen Bill's inside and his inside seen me. So

125

I didn't never let his outside self bother me too much. Because I knowed more about him than he knowed about himself. An' I know he loved me. An' he woulda loved Janey too, if he'd ever seen her. Yeah, the three of us would have been a pair.

Anyway, I done a lot of things in my life that Janey wouldn't understand. Hell, I don't understand. But I ain't all as bad as they make me out, either.

You ask who midwifed half the babies in Deadwood. You ask who nursed them folks with smallpox when not one single soul would set foot in the pest house, except yours truly. Them women all the time actin' uppity-up 'cause I don't look all frilly and smell like roses, but you ask 'em if they wasn't damn glad I didn't care what my face looked like when they was needin' somebody to nurse 'em through smallpox. Ask 'em.

You tell Janey her mother done some good things. Done some bad ones too. Sometimes you catch the chicken and sometimes you jes' git the feathers. But you tell her that whatever people say about her mother, she can hold her head up high, 'cause her daddy was James Butler Hickok.

She pronounces his name slowly and defiantly. She waits for a moment, as if daring the audience to challenge her. Satisfied she's made her point, she turns back to the flask for a final swallow before screwing the top back on and replacing it in her boot. Heaving herself out of the chair, she lumbers offstage.

THE END

Cookin' With Typhoid Mary

COOKIN' WITH TYPHOID MARY

The scene is a large, but shabby institutional kitchen. In the center of the stage is a long table with a cutting board and a huge institutional cooking pot. There are sacks of potatoes, onions, and tomatoes scattered on the table and the floor surrounding it. A tall stool stands to one side of the table.

MARY MALLON is cooking. Mary is a large Irish woman of forty-five, with beefy arms. She wears a cheap dress from 1914, with a soiled apron over it. As the play opens, Mary is chopping a potato to throw in the pot. She uses an enormous knife, and sings while she works:

WE HAVE A LOYAL LITTLE FRIEND
THE POTATO SMOOTH AND ROUND,
AND SELDOM DOES IT FAIL TO LEND,
A DISH THAT'S GOOD AND SOUND . . .

[*Mary stops abruptly, noticing the audience.*] There wouldn't be a George Soper here, would there? A "Doctor" George Soper? Nasty little pig-eyed bastard holdin' his hat over his privates like he's got somethin' to be ashamed of, which he does! [*Looking around*] No? Well, if he comes in, you'll tell me, won't you? I've got a little present for him. [*She picks up the large knife again and resumes chopping.*] And you don't need to be starin' at me like you don't know who I am. Mary Mallon. Mary Mallon of Tuxedo Park, Oyster Island, Park Avenue and Riverside. Don't tell me you never heard the name? Mary Mallon. The finest cook in Manhattan. The one they all ask for when they go to the agencies. That's me. Mary Mallon. [*She lifts the knife to chop a potato, but stops in mid-*

swing to inspect it.] Now, you don't want to be cuttin' this one. See how green the end is? That means it wasn't deep enough in the ground. You've got to bury them good while they're young, or they turn out bitter, don't you know? [*She tosses it to the side.*] So you're askin' yourself what a fine woman like Mary Mallon is doin' in this dungeon of a kitchen, slavin' away at a pile of potatoes, and only herself to be doin' the work of a dozen. You're askin' yourself who's responsible for her bein' in this hell-hole, and I'll tell you. It was that devil of a doctor, George Soper. Him and his hat and what's under it. [*She chops with a vengeance and picks up the pieces to throw in the pot, when suddenly something on one of the pieces catches her eye.*]

Will you look at this! Eyes as big as a baby's finger. [*She begins to "eye" the potato pieces.*] Them eyes is really sprouts, you know. If you have a potato long enough, them little eyes grows hands and starts feelin' their way towards the light, and then you've got trouble. One day you open up the cabinet for your sack of potatoes, and there they are—hundreds of gropin' little pale hands, stretchin' themselves out to you, just beggin' for a touch of sunlight. And you can't have that! [*She whacks the cutting board with the knife, and then laughs at her own violence.*]

It takes food to be growin' them little hands. You can't be lettin' them little eyes see too much, or the next thing you know they'll be stealing the potato for themselves, instead of leavin' it for them that paid for it, the way God meant it to be. So you've got to poke them out—like this. [*She gouges a potato eye with her knife.*]

Now, if I was cookin' for them rich folks still, I'd be peelin' the skins off, too. That's how them rich folks like their potatoes—all pale and smooth, like them pictures of naked women they got hangin' on their walls. Like they was made up in heaven by God himself and flown to earth by the angels. Like a potato didn't come up out of the ground rough and dirty like them that dug it up. They don't like to think about things like that, them rich folks. And why should they? They're never goin' to look down on that fancy silver platter and see a potato sittin' there, black with blight, crumblin' to pieces when you touch it, like a rotten tooth in an old man's head. [*She whacks another potato and begins to sing:*]

WE HAVE A LOYAL LITTLE FRIEND
THE POTATO SMOOTH AND ROUND,
AND SELDOM DOES IT FAIL TO LEND,
A DISH THAT'S GOOD AND SOUND.
OH! TRULY TIS A FRIEND IN NEED
THO TREATED WITH DISDAIN,
A MOST ESSENTIAL FOOD INDEED,
THAT FULLY EARNS ITS FAME.

My mother taught me that. She was from Galway. [*She inspects a potato.*] Galway was the worst, you know. She said there wasn't a single potato in the whole county that didn't have the blight. That was in '49. She said they was eatin' 'em anyway, black spots and all. But then, a rotten potato's not such a bad thing when you're cookin' up grass and seaweed to keep yourself alive. You see, there wasn't any grain or livestock left, because our landlords had come all the way over from England—in the spirit of Christian charity, don't you know—just to buy us out . . . [*Turning her attention back to the potato*] Not that we weren't dyin' to sell. [*She chops it.*]

She was a fierce one, my mother. Told my da he could go to hell or stay in Dublin—it was all the same to her, but she was takin' her daughter where there was more to live for than watchin' your babies starve while you worked yourself to death. I never saw my da again—not that I'd have known it if I stepped on him. My mother borrowed the money to buy us a passage in steerage—just her and myself. And that's how we left, just the two of us. [*She takes out an onion and begins to peel it.*]

Well, she took sick on the crossin'. We all did. All of us that was in steerage. First you get the fever, and then you get the cramps, and then you go to passin' blood, and then you die—unless you live, which is just as bad as dyin' if you're down in steerage. And then they come and fetch your body and heave it over the side, like it was a sack of potatoes. Only, of course, they'd never throw a perfectly fine sack of potatoes into the water. [*She laughs.*] There's nothing like an onion to bring a tear to Mary Mallon's eye! [*She wipes her eyes and chops the onion.*]

But I was tellin' you about the crossin'. We both took sick together, and there we lay, the two of us, under the blankets, shiverin' and crampin' and wishin' we were rich enough to be makin' the crossin' in one of them heated cabins with a bed and a toilet and running water like them folks that leaned over the railin's in the daytime and tossed oranges at us like we were animals in a pit. And then one night, I'm lyin' with my mother and listenin' to the wailin' of a baby and thinkin' what a blessin' that it still had the strength to cry—when all of a sudden my mother grabs at me and starts openin' her mouth, and then just as sudden she closes it again, and she drops back beside me, and I ask her what she's seen, but she's not sayin' anything to me, and I feel her fingers lettin' go of my arm, so now it's me that's grabbin' onto her—and she's not movin' at all. She's not sayin' a word. Not makin' a bloody sound. And then I start to feel her legs against my feet, gettin' colder and colder. [*She wipes her eyes from the onions.*]

So, what do I do? I start hailin' Mary, full of grace, that's what I do. [*She laughs.*] And when that doesn't work, I hail her again, and then again, and again! And you know, that's how they found us. My mother stiff as a poker, and dead for two days, and me clingin' to her like a barnacle and saying my Hail Marys like I'm racing the devil to beat her to heaven. [*She laughs again.*]

Well, they had a time of it, gettin' her body. They sent down the ship's doctor, don't you know. And the only time the bastard ever set foot in steerage, was to come down and count up the dead. And here he is leanin' over me, tryin' to get a peek at my poor mother's face—and I jump on him like a cat guardin' her kittens, scratchin' and clawin' at his pasty white face, just tryin' to see what he would be lookin' like when he was dead! [*She laughs.*]

It took 'em four men to fetch my mother's body—and three of them was just to get me off the doctor. [*She resumes chopping the onion.*]

Of course, I lied about my age when we landed. I wasn't about to give them another chance to be feedin' Mary Mallon's body to the seagulls. [*She stops and looks at the audience.*]

So now you're askin' yourself how a little girl, without a penny in her purse and not knowin' a livin' soul on the continent, managed to keep herself from starvin' to death. Well, you figure it out. You'd be surprised how much work there is for a little girl in New York. [*She throws the onion in the pot.*]

He hasn't come in, has he? That devil of a doctor, Soper . . . ? You will tell me, if he comes in now? [*She pulls a tomato out of one of the sacks.*]

You know the secret of cuttin' tomatoes? You slide the tip of the blade up under the skin just before you cut, and that way it won't spit the juice all over you. [*She begins to slice tomatoes. She becomes more and more aggressive, reducing the tomatoes to a mound of red pulp.*]

You know, people used to believe tomatoes was poison. I read it in the paper. It took a hundred years for some brave soul to get up the courage to eat one. Can you imagine it? Thinkin' a tomato was poison! Now, I ask you, what would give a body an idea like that about a tomato? Well, I'll tell you. Some poor woman cooked up a tomato one day, and then some rich old bastard had it for his dinner, and died in his sleep on account of his sins, and then don't you know, they go lookin' for the cook who must have done him in, because rich folks don't like to believe they have to die same as the poor and that for all their money, they can't bribe their way out of death like they can out of prison. No, they can't believe that, so they have to go out and find somebody to pin it on. And like as not the woman's Irish. And there you are—tomatoes are poison. And the next thing you know, it's in all the papers, and they start callin' her Tomato Mary. And then there's a dozen folks from all over New York, who suddenly remember hirin' a cook whose name was Mary, and that somebody somewhere died sometime after eatin' at their table. And then the whole world is hearin' of New York's tomato epidemic. And that poor woman's spendin' her life in hidin' or in jail for the ignorance and arrogance of the bloody rich who think they can buy their way out of everything. Well, just maybe it wasn't the tomatoes killed them. Maybe it was their own wretched lies pilin' up on their souls till they collapse in on them like a roof on rotted timbers. [*She grabs handfuls of the tomato pulp and dumps them into the pot as she sings:*]

THEY SAY SIR WALTER RALEIGH
[SO IT'S GENERALLY AGREED]
IMPLANTED IN OUR VALLEYS FAIR
THE FIRST PROLIFIC SEED.
THERE SPRANG FROM FERTILE SOIL
[AT LEAST THAT'S WHAT WE'RE TOLD]
WITH EAGER CARE AND EARNEST TOIL
A CROP A HUNDRED-FOLD

[*She goes back to chopping potatoes.*] Sir Walter Raleigh. He would be an Englishman, now, wouldn't he? A gentleman, too. And, look, he's bringin' a little souvenir from America over to Ireland! Now, isn't that kind of him, to be thinkin' of his neighbors and bringin' them the marvelous little potato? They say you can grow six wagonloads on one acre! And they say you can grow it in any kind of dirt! Now, isn't that a wonder? And why should a body be wastin' time and trouble with the likes of sheep, when for half the land and twice the money, you can be growin' the marvelous potato? So now all of Ireland starts sellin' off their land in great chunks and breedin' themselves like prize bulls, until there's four times the people livin' on twice the farms, if you can call five acres a farm. [*She becomes increasingly frenzied with her chopping as she speaks.*]

Ah, the marvelous potato. "Sir" Walter Raleigh never told us the potato would fail. He never told us it would fail five years in a row. He never told us he was bringin' death to Ireland, sowin' potatoes in the ground like they was the dragon's teeth in the story, and that everywhere he planted one, there would be springin' up a skeleton until Ireland was a land of corpses. No, he never told us that, did he? I'm sure "Sir" Walter Raleigh never dreamed his little potato was goin' to invade the Irish like a murderin' army of heathens—now did he? I'm sure no one ever accused him of killin' a single person, did they? I'm sure they never tried to lock him up for bein' a "potato carrier." But then, he was an Englishman, wasn't he? [*She wipes her hands on her apron, collecting herself.*]

You know I'm not usin' my real name here. I'm goin' by "Mary Brown." They're not goin' to find me here. Soper can look as hard as he wants, but he's never goin' to find me. I've picked the best place to hide in New York. [*She crosses down to the stool.*] Soper—and a slimier little bastard you never saw. First time I laid eyes on him, he's standin' in the kitchen where I was workin'—got someone to show him in, the weasel did, and he's standin' there with his hat in his hand, in front of him like this, you know. You know how them gents do that. Hold it right here like they've got something to hide—which most of them do. And he calls out "Mary." And I look up like it should be someone that knows me, either that or someone who's hired me. But instead, I see this nasty little bastard—him and his little piggy eyes. And he's tellin' me he's from the city health department. And then he starts talkin' about little invisible animals, and I'm thinkin' it's on account of my bein' Irish—you know, the "little people," and all. So I tell Dr. Soper I'm a busy woman and if he'll get along with his business, then I'll be gettin' along with mine. Do you know what he does then? He looks me square in the eye and says, "Mary!"—not "Miss Mallon," mind you, but "Mary!" He says, "Mary! I want your blood, your urine, and your feces." Stood right there in the kitchen, he did, and said it just like he was goin' over the menu. "Your blood, your urine, and your feces." And then he takes a step towards me, so I grab up the carvin' fork, like this . . . [*She demonstrates with the knife.*] . . . and I let him know what I think of him and his filthy mouth. I guess he sees who's goin' to be gettin' whose blood if it came to that, because he takes off runnin' down the hall, out the door, through the gate, and off down the sidewalk. You watch 'em when they hold their hats like that. [*She sets the knife down.*]

Now, you'd think that would be the end of Dr. Soper, but there's some of them that's been at their business so long, they've got no shame. He tracks me 'round to my roomin' house. I was livin' on Third Avenue, you know, there below 33rd Street. It was a decent place, I'll have you know. And this Soper, he's got a friend with him, and the two of them are waitin' on the landin' for me, at the top of the stairs, talkin' loud enough for all the tenants in the buildin' to hear, and this time he asks me if I'm in the habit of washin' my hands after I go to the toilet! [*She returns to chopping her potatoes.*]

If you're a woman and you're Irish, they think they can say anything they like, and you've got to take it. Not this woman. Not Mary Mallon. I haven't lived through what I've lived through to be subjectin' myself to that kind of filth. I let the whole roomin' house know what I thought of that pair! Well, now, don't you see, I've humiliated him in front of his friend. Now he's goin' to be havin' to arrest me. [*Crossing back to the stool*]

But does he do his own dirty work? Not his kind! No, he goes out and gets himself a woman for the job. A Dr. S. Josephine Baker. And a fine one she was—wearin' a jacket and a tie like she was a man. Had her hair all combed back like one, too. [*Mary shakes her head.*]

She was a tricky one. The first time I found out her business, I slammed the door in her face. So then she comes back, her and three police officers. And this time, she goes around to the servant's entrance in the basement and rings the bell, so I won't suspect it was them. As soon as I see who it is, I try to slam the door, but one of the police has already got his bloody foot in the door. So I run back upstairs, and here's another peeler at the front door! So I go back to the kitchen and climb out the window. There's a fence between this house and the one next to it, so I pull a chair to it and climb over. And there's a little shed built into the back of the house, so I go in there and hide, pullin' the ash cans to the door, so they won't suspect I'm in there. So here's poor Mary Mallon, crouchin' for three hours in the freezin' cold, no jacket—and just when I'm thinkin' it might be safe to come out, that bloodhound of a doctor spots a bit of my dress from under the door. And they come after me—her and the three peelers. Well, I give them a run for their money—just like I done on that ship—kickin' and bitin' even after they get my arms pinned back. Kicked one of them peelers so hard, he said his equipment would never work again! [*She chops a potato.*]

Well, don't you know, they've hired an ambulance so it looks like they're public officials doin' their duty by takin' a poor crazy woman away, instead of criminals kidnappin' an honest citizen on account of that dirty-minded bastard Soper. And Dr. S. Josephine Baker—she was sittin' on top of me the whole ride! [*Chopping again*]

And they lock me in a hospital room. It's like a peeled potato, this room is. White walls, white ceiling, white floor. And they take my clothes and they give me a white bathrobe. And they keep checkin' the bedpan every few hours. I know what they want. Didn't that bastard Soper stand right there and tell me to my face? I've seen his kind. So I'm tryin' not to oblige, but nature's not friendly. And of course, they come and take the pot away now. So then after I'm in this hell-hole for a while, the little bastard himself decides to show himself. He comes in and stands in front of the door, in case he might have to leave in a hurry. So, he's standin' like this with his back to the door. And he's talkin' to me like I'm a misbehavin' child and he's my da, and that I've done somethin' he ought to forgive me for. He's goin' on about them invisible things again—only now he's more excited, because he's got what he wanted from me, and he's tellin' me the invisible things is crawlin' all over—and he tells me that when I go to the toilet, they crawl up my hands and then, if I don't wash them off, they crawl onto the food and people eat them and die! And then he gets onto what really excites him—my gall bladder. So then I know the bastard intends to murder me. He tells me the invisible things is all livin' up my gall bladder—but he's goin' to be kind enough to cut open my body and take it out for me. Well, I'm not fool enough to sign my own death certificate, thank you very much. [*Crossing down front*]

What do I do? I get up out of the bed, which is the only furniture in the room, and I'm lookin' at him the whole time—starin' him right in his little piggy eye, the bloody bastard—and I take my time walkin' to the

137

bathroom, just like I was in my own house . . . And then I slam the door hard enough to be heard in hell! Twice more the little bastard tried to get me to give him my gall bladder. Bastard. No good talkin' to the people who brought me food. They were all workin' for him. Thought he was a bleedin' genius with his ideas about little invisible animals crawlin' around makin' people sick. So then they move me to another hospital—out on North Brother Island. Right in the middle of the East River, off 138th Street. They called it an "isolation center." I spent three years in that place. Three years never gettin' to be with anybody. Them just bringin' my meals to the door and shovin' them in, and then runnin' away like I was some kind of leper. Me, never sick a day in my life— except for the fever on the crossin'—and that was just bein' in steerage. [*She crosses back to the potatoes and picks one up thoughtfully.*]

They let me out four years ago. Somebody must have gotten tired of Soper and his stories. Or maybe Soper gave up on havin' my gall bladder. But of course, they had to do it up official, like they hadn't kidnapped me. I'm supposed to be reportin' to them on my "activities" every three months. [*She laughs.*]

Made me sign a paper that I'd never cook for a livin' again. Now that was charitable of them, don't you think? Maybe they was hopin' I'd hire on as the president of a bank. [*She laughs again.*]

They fix it so there's only two ways a woman can get by, don't you know. Them Sopers of the world. [*She hacks a potato.*] I'm a cook. I made good money, too. Of course, I was goin' back to it. But then I find out that Soper's been to the agencies. The little bastard went to Stricker's and Seeley's and took 'em my picture, and told them all about my gall bladder. Can you believe it? The only two agencies in New York, and so now I can't get on. Bastard! [*She chops potatoes.*]

Death. Them rich folks will spend a pot of money lookin' for it. Makin' up fairy stories, huntin' down innocent people. They go trackin' down death like it was some kind of mystery. Didn't a million people starve to death in Ireland while the rest of the world stood around biddin' over the bones? Didn't my own mother die the death of a dog on that ship while the rich folks looked down over their railin's at us like we were just so many animals in a filthy cage? And where is the city in the world that doesn't have a street for the buyin' of a girl's body and the sellin' of her soul? You don't need a microscope to see death. [*She holds up a potato.*]

It's as big and as plain as a potato. [*She laughs.*]

But I'll tell you a secret. They'll never come lookin' for me here—the Sloan Hospital. Dr. George Soper and his cronies wouldn't be caught dead in this place! [*She whispers.*] Do you know why? It's a public maternity hospital. [*She throws back her head and shouts.*] There's nobody here but poor women and their starvin' babies! [*She laughs uproariously. The lights fade to the sound of her laughter.*]

THE END

139

Original Cast Lists

All performances were produced by No to Men Productions at Positively Fourth Street, Ashland, Oregon, under the direction of Carolyn Gage.

The Second Coming of Joan of Arc—November 24, 1989
    Jeanne Romée—Carolyn Gage

Mason-Dixon—March 23, 1990
    Mary Elizabeth Bowser—Jolie Johnson
    Elizabeth Van Lew—Carolyn Gage

Jane Addams and the Devil Baby—March 23, 1990
    Jane Addams—Judy Kaplan
    Mary Rozet Smith—Natalie Garrett
    Kathleen—Wyrda

Louisa May Incest—March 23, 1990
    Louisa May Alcott—Michaelia Morgan
    Jo March—Sue Carney

Battered on Broadway—March 23, 1990
    Nellie Forbush Debecque—Michaelia Morgan
    Bess—Jolie Johnson
    Mei Li—Hyacinth Ware
    Aldonza—Clara Bellone
    Maria—Genoveva Wise
    Julie Jordan—Natalie Garrett
    Sally Bowles—Akia Woods
    Orphan Annie—Wyrda
    Maid—Carolyn Gage
    Nun—Natalie Garrett

Calamity Jane Sends a Message to Her Daughter—June 29, 1989
    Calamity Jane—Brandy Carson

Cookin' with Typhoid Mary—July 20, 1990
    Mary Mallon—Wyrda

Information on Production Rights

The author of these plays is a member of the Dramatists Guild, and she uses a modified version of the Guild's production contract to license all performances and readings of her work. This contract specifies the terms for royalties, as well as for affirmative action casting, publicity, script revision, videotaping, and other aspects pertinent to production.

The contract must be signed by both parties prior to the production date, otherwise the production constitutes an infringement of the playwright's copyright and is subject to legal sanctions. Technically everyone associated with an unauthorized production (actors, producers, directors) is liable for the playwright's damages and legal expenses. All productions must be licensed, whether or not admission is charged (festivals, conferences, public readings).

In order to review the production contract or discuss production plans, you may contact the playwright care of HerBooks, P.O. Box 7467, Santa Cruz, CA, 95061.

For the Audio-Cassette Recording
of Carolyn Gage in
in *The Second Coming of Joan of Arc*
recorded live at the Institute for the Musical Arts
with an introduction by June Millington
send $12.00 to Carolyn Gage
c/o HerBooks, P.O. Box 7467, Santa Cruz, CA 95061

For a complete catalogue of Gage's monologues, one-acts, musicals, and full-length dramas send $2.00 to Carolyn Gage c/o HerBooks.